What readers are saying about In

Google Drive & Docs In 30 Minutes

"I bought your Google Docs guide myself (my new company uses it) and it was really handy. I loved it."

"I have been impressed by the writing style and how easy it was to get very familiar and start leveraging Google Docs. I can't wait for more titles. Nice job!"

Genealogy Basics In 30 Minutes

"This basic genealogy book is a fast, informative read that will get you on your way if you are ready to begin your genealogy journey or are looking for tips to push past a problem area."

"The personal one-on-one feel and the obvious dedication it took to boil down a lot of research into such a small book and still make it readable are the two reasons I give this book such a high rating. Recommended."

Crowdfunding Basics In 30 Minutes

"Very understandable and absorbing. A must-read for any entrepreneur."

"On the verge of launching a crowdfunding campaign myself, this book has made me re-think my plans and my strategy. Take a step back and get the advice of someone who's been there."

Twitter In 30 Minutes

"A perfect introduction to Twitter. Quick and easy read with lots of photos. I finally understand the # symbol!"

"Clarified any issues and concerns I had and listed some excellent precautions."

Excel Basics In 30 Minutes

"Fast and easy. The material presented is very basic but it is also accessible with step-by-step screenshots and a friendly tone more like a friend or co-worker explaining how to use Excel than a technical manual."

"An excellent little guide. For those who already know their way around Excel, it'll be a good refresher course. Definitely plan on passing it around the office."

Learn more about In 30 Minutes® guides at in30minutes.com

PowerPoint Basics

In 30 Minutes

How to make effective PowerPoint presentations using a PC, Mac, PowerPoint Online, or the PowerPoint app

By Angela Rose

In 30 Minutes® Guides
QUICK GUIDES FOR A COMPLEX WORLD®
in30minutes.com

PowerPoint Basics In 30 Minutes
ISBN: 978-1-939924-85-8
Library of Congress Control Number: 2017957944
Copyright © 2017 by i30 Media Corporation.

Cover and interior design *by* Monica Thomas for TLC Graphics, www.TLCGraphics.com. Interior design and composition assisted *by* Rick Soldin, book-comp.com.

Contents

Contents

Contents

Introduction

A 30-year-old communication powerhouse

It was 1984—the year I turned 12 and developed my first serious crush. While I was spending my free time pedaling laps around the neighborhood on my bicycle just so I could ride by a certain boy's house, computer scientists Robert Gaskins and Dennis Austin were launching the software program that eventually became Microsoft PowerPoint. Originally known as *Presenter,* Gaskins and Austin designed it to modernize the process of creating old-fashioned projection slides, and bring presentations into the 20th century.

At a time when my pre-teen allowance was a mere $3 per week, Gaskin and Austin's program raked in $1 million in its first month. By the time Power-Point celebrated its 30th birthday, it was estimated that more than 1 billion copies of the software had been sold. The day I turned 45 (celebrating that milestone with tacos, of course), PowerPoint users around the globe created more than 30 million presentations—colloquially known as "PowerPoints" or "decks"—in 24 hours.

When you think about communicating ideas and information to a group of people in a room or venue, it's easy to understand why so many people choose PowerPoint for their presentations. In fact, according to the Social Science Research Network, visual learners, or people who need to see what they are learning in order to understand and absorb it, make up 65 percent of the population.

I began to use PowerPoint more than a decade ago, while working as a creative department manager at a small marketing company. Our clients, who were primarily mortgage and real estate agents, wanted an effective way to educate their customers on various homeownership topics. We began to design customizable PowerPoint presentations on exciting subjects such as the mortgage application process, fixed-rate versus adjustable rate loans, and real estate taxes.

There are many more possibilities for using PowerPoint. Over the years, I've encountered the following types of presentations, both in person and online:

➤ University lectures

➤ Doctors' salaries

➤ Pharmaceutical research methods

➤ Early Edwardian fashion

➤ The health benefits of turmeric

➤ The history of the soufflé

➤ How to irrigate your sinuses

However, as a crazy cat lady in training, my favorite PowerPoint presentations of late are those created by a feline rescue organization in Canada. Configured to autoplay and be shared online, the presentations focus on spaying and neutering, as well as the value of feral and formerly feral felines. While the presentations range from amusing to moving, they are always informative and memorable—as every truly great PowerPoint must be.

How people use PowerPoint

As I mentioned earlier, it has been estimated (by Microsoft) that people around the world create tens of millions of PowerPoint presentations every day. Because it's such a versatile visual communication tool, people find all kinds of uses for the software. Here are just a few examples:

➤ **Oscar has a great idea for a new company and needs to pitch it to investors**. It has been a few years since he last worked with

PowerPoint, so he purchased this book to help him create a presentation to illustrate his business plan which he can use in meetings to engage bankers or potential investors.

➤ **Martha is the manager of a growing dental office.** She recently realized she needs a bigger budget for office supplies. She is using a PowerPoint presentation to outline the areas in which her current budget is falling short, as well as show how a greater investment in these resources will improve staff productivity.

➤ **Norbert is a high school history teacher and uses PowerPoint in his classroom.** Familiar with the numerous studies on visual learning, he creates presentations that review essential information before final exams. Because he often goes six months or more between presentations, he refers to this book whenever he needs to refresh his knowledge of the software's basic features.

➤ **Robin loves cats and has taken it upon herself to care for a colony of strays in her neighborhood.** Unfortunately, the local homeowners' association wants to trap and destroy them. She is using PowerPoint to create a compelling presentation about trap, neuter, and release programs that she can share at the next association meeting. This book will help her avoid common pitfalls that could reduce the effectiveness of her slide deck.

➤ **Barbara is a scientist who works for the U.S. Centers for Disease Control and Prevention (CDC).** Her assistant, who usually puts together the department's research summaries, is on family leave. Because the budget won't support hiring a temporary replacement, Barbara plans to use PowerPoint on her own to share research updates with upper management.

➤ **Jordan is a computer-savvy 9-year-old and he really, really, really wants a dog.** When regular whining didn't work, he decided to put together a PowerPoint presentation to teach his parents about all the reasons why he should have a dog and what he'll do to help take care of it if he gets a puppy for his birthday.

PowerPoint can be a complex software application. We won't be getting into all of the tools and advanced features. However, if you're a novice user or just want a quick refresher, then you will find lots to love in this guide. It contains plenty of step-by-step instructions and screenshots to get you going, as well as protips and best practices to nudge you toward the next level. Topics include:

➤ Navigating PowerPoint's Ribbon.

➤ How to create a new presentation.

➤ Adding, copying, and reordering slides.

➤ Formatting text, backgrounds, and more.

➤ Adding cool effects such as transitions and animations.

➤ How to save, print, export, and present PowerPoint slide decks.

You'll learn all of this in about 30 minutes. That's less time than it takes to bake a cake. If you're ready, let's get started!

CHAPTER 1

Choosing, launching, and navigating PowerPoint

When I began working with PowerPoint presentations more than 10 years ago, our office was equipped with an old PC version of the software. Even then it was a powerful program, capable of creating presentations with images, text, and even the occasional animation.

While nearly every iteration since has added new features, some of the most substantial changes have been visual. PowerPoint 2010 included early collaboration features, and also introduced the Ribbon interface (which replaced the toolbars) as well as Backstage View (which eliminated the File menu). These interface elements are shared with other programs in the Microsoft Office suite, such as Microsoft Word and Excel, so if you use those programs, the PowerPoint interface will seem familiar.

PowerPoint 2013 added new design themes, tools to merge shapes, and improved collaboration tools. With the most recent release of PowerPoint 2016, users were introduced to the Tell Me tool, new chart types, screen recording, real-time collaboration, and more. But that's not all: Microsoft's developers continue to refine the program, releasing new versions of the build several times a year.

What does this mean for you? Basically, if you've used a previous version of the software, many of the tools you'll encounter while working with Power-Point 2016 will be familiar, and will work in much the same way as they have in the past. There will be some cool new features to incorporate into your presentations. And those of you who are completely new to PowerPoint can rest assured that you have nothing to fear. Even a beginner will find the software simple to navigate and easy to use.

PowerPoint purchase options

This edition of *PowerPoint Basics In 30 Minutes* was written primarily for the 2016 desktop version of the software for Windows PCs and Macs. However, it's possible to access a free (but limited) version of the software via a web browser called PowerPoint Online. There are also PowerPoint apps for Android and iOS devices. Most of the instructions and examples in this guide will refer to PowerPoint 2016 for Windows and macOS, but there are also tips for using PowerPoint Online and the PowerPoint mobile apps.

There are two main differences between the desktop version of PowerPoint and PowerPoint Online: cost and functionality.

PowerPoint vs. PowerPoint Online: Cost

As of this writing, it is still possible to purchase a copy of the most recent version of PowerPoint (to install on a single PC) for a little over $100. PowerPoint is also part of the Microsoft Office 2016 software suite, which costs about $230.

However, these options may not be available forever. In recent years, Microsoft has been pushing customers to subscribe to PowerPoint and other programs in the Office family. You can subscribe to Office 365 Home for about $10 per month and get PowerPoint along with Word, Excel, OneNote, and Publisher for up to five PCs, five tablets and five smartphones. If you're a business user, Office 365 Business is also available for about $10 per month/per user. If you're interested in trying out Office 365 Business, Microsoft offers a free trial.

I found the Office 365 Home subscription to be the best deal for my purposes. Not only can you share unused installations with friends and family members, but the software suite will also automatically update whenever a new version is released, for as long as you maintain your subscription. (To put this in perspective, Microsoft released three build updates in the first nine months of 2017. If I weren't an Office 365 subscriber, I would have missed out on a lot of new features and enhancements.)

To start a subscription, simply visit office.microsoft.com and select the version of Office 365 you want to use. You will need to register for a Microsoft account, activate the subscription, and download and install the entire Office suite, which includes the most recent version of PowerPoint. It is possible to turn off the subscription if you do not anticipate using it for a few months, and then reactivate it later.

PowerPoint Online, on the other hand, is totally free. That may sound wonderful, but "free" comes at a cost—in this case, reduced functionality.

> **Protip:** You already have a Microsoft account if you use Xbox Live, Skype, Hotmail, or practically any other Microsoft-owned service that requires registration. You can use the same login credentials to start an Office 365 subscription or use PowerPoint Online. You can also create a new Microsoft account.

PowerPoint vs. PowerPoint Online: Functionality

The latest desktop version of PowerPoint is a powerhouse, developed and improved over several decades. As you will learn over the chapters that follow, the features are extensive and can help you create amazing presentations. For example, here is the selection of tools available on the Insert tab of PowerPoint's Ribbon.

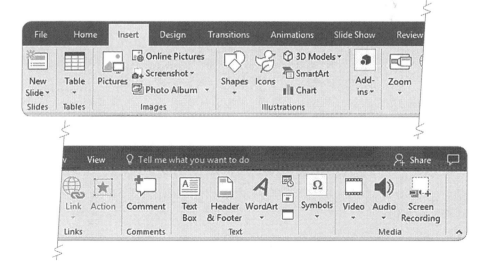

PowerPoint Online, on the other hand, is a stripped-down version of the software that has been available for a much shorter period. It opens up in a web browser, but it contains a thin selection of formatting and design tools. As you can see in this screenshot, the Insert tab on PowerPoint Online's Ribbon contains far fewer options.

While most of the tools work the same way, using PowerPoint Online will limit the types of presentations you can create because many features are not available. In addition, you can only use PowerPoint Online when you have Internet access. This means that if you are on a long-distance flight, you will probably be unable to use PowerPoint Online to edit your sales presentation. You also cannot use PowerPoint Online in a coffee shop, hotel room, or at home unless you are connected to the Internet.

If you want to try PowerPoint Online, go to office.live.com and log in, or register using your Microsoft account.

Mobile apps for Android and iOS

The PowerPoint apps for Android and iOS devices have an impressive feature set, but are limited by the small screen size, a lack of a real keyboard, and issues associated with saving local files. The apps allow you to make new presentations, edit presentations you've previously created, and even present your PowerPoint slide deck using PowerPoint Online.

The apps are available for free on Google Play (Android phones and tablets) and the App Store (iOS devices such as the iPhone and iPad). However, if you want to unlock full functionality, you'll need to purchase an Office 365 subscription.

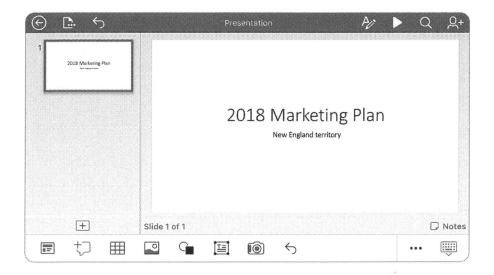

The mobile apps are good for reviewing presentations already stored on the device and making basic edits. They are less useful for creating presentations from scratch, unless you have a wireless keyboard and access to images and other files that you might want to incorporate into the presentation.

In the chapters that follow, I will mostly refer to the desktop version of PowerPoint for Windows and macOS, as well as certain features that are available in PowerPoint Online and the mobile apps for Android and iOS.

OneDrive

With the latest version of PowerPoint, Microsoft has increased integration with OneDrive, the company's cloud storage service that was formerly branded as SkyDrive. The service is free to use with a Microsoft account, although greater amounts of storage will be allocated to Office 365 Home and Office 365 Business users. PowerPoint files saved to OneDrive are synchronized over the Internet to remote server farms operated by Microsoft. There are several advantages associated with saving a file to OneDrive:

➤ Files can be accessed from any logged-in PC or mobile device.

➤ Even if your computer breaks down or is stolen, files on OneDrive can still be opened using another computer or device.

➤ OneDrive enables you to share your PowerPoint presentation with others—such as coworkers who need to review your work—without the need for you to print or email the file.

There are some drawbacks to OneDrive. Most importantly, the service requires Wi-Fi or a network connection to sync files. In addition, OneDrive's syncing and cross-platform abilities are not as slick as those of Dropbox and other cloud storage services.

OneDrive is required if you are using PowerPoint Online, but if you have the desktop version of PowerPoint, it's easy enough to save to your local hard drive. The PowerPoint mobile apps for Android and iOS devices can save to OneDrive or to the device's storage as long as enough space is available to do so.

Launching PowerPoint

To get started with PowerPoint, click the PowerPoint 2016 icon on your desktop, dock, or in your applications folder. To launch PowerPoint Online, go to office.live.com. If you're not already logged in, the interface will prompt you to enter your Microsoft account information.

The first thing that appears after the program launches is the Start Screen. The Start Screen is divided into a list of recent presentations (the left third of the screen) and the new presentation gallery (the right two-thirds of the screen).

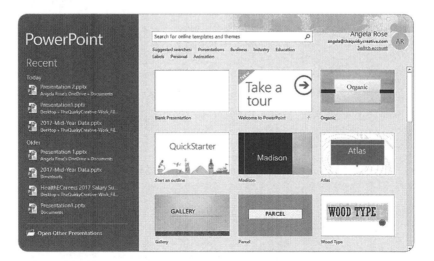

From the Start Screen, you can take the following actions:

➤ **Open an existing presentation.** If you want to resume working on a previously created presentation, you can look for it in the Recent Presentations list. Within this list, PowerPoint includes presentations you were working on in recent days and weeks. Simply click on the presentation you want to access or, if it's not listed, choose *Open Other Presentations* at the bottom of the list (Windows) or *Open from One-Drive* (PowerPoint Online). You can then navigate to the document's location on your computer or on OneDrive if you have saved it to Microsoft's cloud.

➤ **Open a blank presentation.** If you want to start a fresh presentation from scratch, simply select the blank presentation thumbnail in the new document gallery.

➤ **Open a new presentation with a pre-designed template or theme.** All versions of PowerPoint include a library of templates and themes to jumpstart your design. These include business-appropriate templates as well as themes designed for more informal use. Thumbnails are displayed in the new presentation gallery. Browse by category or enter keywords into the search bar. Then just click the thumbnail to start a new presentation.

Protip: Some experts advise against relying on PowerPoint's prebuilt templates and themes, especially if your goal is to create a presentation that is unique to your purposes. However, working with a template or prebuilt theme is an easy way to familiarize yourself with the different elements and options at your disposal. They can also save a lot of time!

It's possible to launch PowerPoint by opening an existing presentation from your hard drive using File Explorer (Windows) or Finder (macOS). You won't see the Start Screen, but you can get to Backstage View (which includes options to open recent files, create new files, and perform other tasks) by selecting *File* at the top of the screen.

You also won't see the Start Screen if you begin a new document while you are already working on an existing one. In either of these cases, you can get to the new document gallery through PowerPoint's Backstage View. Just select *File* (at the top of the screen) and then *New* (from the Backstage View menu on the left).

PowerPoint Online can only be launched from a browser and can only open presentations that are stored in OneDrive or on Dropbox.

Presenting to an audience

Once your slide show is complete and has been reviewed and signed-off on by any collaborators, managers, or clients, it's time to present it to your audience. You may choose different settings when doing so, depending upon the equipment that is available.

Starting and advancing a presentation

To start your PowerPoint presentation, simply select *From Beginning* on the Slide Show tab or click the Slide Show icon in the Status Bar. Alternatively, you can select *From Current Slide* if you don't want to start at the beginning, but that's an unlikely choice when presenting to an audience.

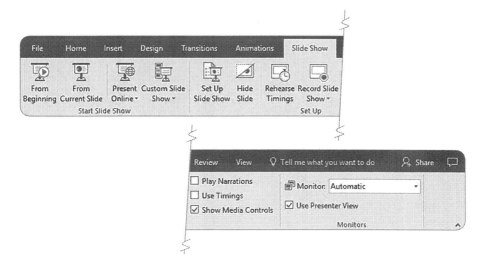

In PowerPoint Online, these controls can be found on the View tab. In the PowerPoint mobile apps, look for the Play icon, which looks like a triangle pointing to the right.

Advance to the next slide by clicking your mouse, pressing the *Spacebar* on your keyboard, pressing the *Right Arrow* key on your keyboard, or by using your mouse to click the Right Arrow icon at the bottom left of your screen. It's also possible to use keyboard shortcuts (see Appendix for Windows and macOS shortcuts).

If you need to reverse slides, use the *Back Arrow* key on your keyboard or click the Back Arrow icon at the bottom left of your screen. You can exit your presentation at any time by pressing the *ESC* key on your keyboard.

If you are using a projector to play your slideshow, here are some handy tips to keep in mind:

➤ Be sure to bring the proper cable to connect your laptop. These vary according to the manufacturer of the laptop and the projector, so check beforehand to make sure you have the right cable.

➤ Don't forget a power cable. Running a presentation on a battery is a recipe for disaster!

➤ Before the slideshow starts, be sure to disable your computer's screen saver or auto-sleep function, so the presentation is not interrupted.

➤ Consider carrying a copy of the presentation on a USB drive (see instructions in Chapter 4) in case you have to use someone else's laptop.

Experienced presenters often have inexpensive hand-held remotes to use with their PowerPoint presentations. A remote typically comes with a small wireless dongle that plugs into a computer's USB port, and doesn't require any special software to use. The remote connects to the dongle via Bluetooth or another wireless technology, and a button on the remote advances the presentation. Some remotes even include laser pointers that let presenters highlight certain items on the projection screens (these are also fun cat toys, incidentally).

If you are playing your presentation on a mobile phone or tablet using the PowerPoint mobile app, swipe to the right to advance the presentation. Transitions and animations will also be activated by swiping.

> **Protip:** As a presenter, you can do more than just advance through each slide. PowerPoint for Windows and macOS also includes drawing tools in the lower left corner of your screen when in Slide Show view. You can use these tools and your mouse to draw on your slides as the presentation is playing. There's even a built-in laser pointer feature that lets you use a mouse to highlight items on the screen.

Using Presenter View

If you're playing your presentation on your laptop but using a projector to create a second display, you may want to consider PowerPoint's *Presenter View* option. Located on the Slide Show tab of the Ribbon, checking the *Presenter View* box will display the full-screen slide show on the second display, while showing a Speaker View on your laptop. The Speaker View includes slide preview, your speaker notes, a timer and more.

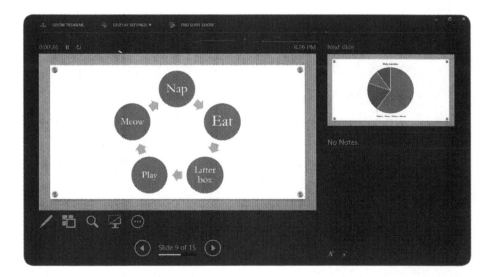

Backstage View

PowerPoint 2016's Backstage View screen is a one-stop shop for many common tasks, including starting new presentations and saving files. Backstage View also includes additional features such as exporting files, printing, and changing certain software settings.

You can get to Backstage View at any time by selecting *File* (Windows or PowerPoint Online) or the File icon (macOS) located at the top left of your screen. Navigating Backstage View is easy, thanks to the simple menu displayed on the left side of the screen:

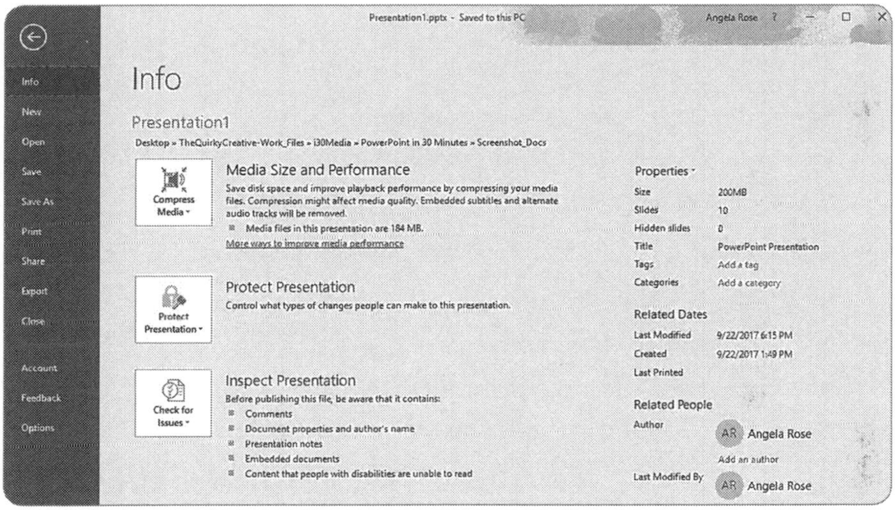

We will go into more detail on many of these menu items later in the book. For the time being, here's a quick overview of the tools in Backstage View for the Windows version of PowerPoint 2016:

➤ **Info.** Review your presentation's properties such as file size and slide count. You can also access tools for protecting, inspecting and managing the presentation. We will dig deeper into the protection options in Chapter 4.

➤ **New.** Start a new presentation from scratch or select a template for customization.

➤ **Open.** Open an existing presentation stored on your computer, network, or the cloud.

➤ **Save and Save As.** Select one of these to save your presentation under its current file name or save a copy in a new location, under a new file name, or as a different file type. We'll talk more about saving files later in this chapter.

➤ **Print.** This is where you will go if you ever want to print your Power-Point presentation. We'll dig deeper into printing in Chapter 4.

➤ **Share.** PowerPoint 2016 has features that enable you to share your presentation with others through the cloud or by email. This is also where you'll find the options for presenting your PowerPoint Online and publishing slides. We'll talk more about much of this in Chapter 4.

➤ **Export.** You can save your presentation as a .pdf document, package your presentation for CD, or create handouts. We'll talk more about exporting in Chapter 4.

➤ **Close.** If you don't want to close your PowerPoint presentation using the "X" in the top-right corner of your screen, you can click *Close* in Backstage View. There are also keyboard shortcuts (see the list in the Appendix).

➤ **Account.** If you have purchased an Office 365 subscription, you can access your account settings and recent updates here.

➤ **Feedback.** The programmers at Microsoft are continually updating the features and functionality of the programs within the Microsoft Office suite, including PowerPoint. If you would like to give them feedback, it's easy to do so here.

➤ **Options.** PowerPoint 2016 includes plenty of settings you can customize to your liking. We'll touch on some of them later in the book.

To exit Backstage View and return to your presentation, simply click on the back arrow at the top of the menu (Windows or PowerPoint Online) or press the *Cancel* button (macOS).

Backstage View for the Mac version of PowerPoint 2016 covers new presentation creation and opening existing files, as well as access to basic account information. However, *Save As*, *Print*, *Share*, *Export*, and *Close* are not visible from the Mac version of Backstage View and have to be accessed via the File drop-down menu at the top of the screen. As for *Options*, many settings in the Mac version of PowerPoint 2016 can be accessed via *PowerPoint > Preferences*.

Navigating PowerPoint's Ribbon interface

PowerPoint 2016 is organized around Microsoft's Ribbon interface and features eight primary tabs, each corresponding to a ribbon-like strip of nifty tools. We will start with a brief overview of what you will find on each tab before digging into specific explanations of the essential features as well as some of the coolest and most useful. Note that there are also several contextual tabs that are hidden from view until certain tools are activated. I will explain some of these later in the book.

➤ **Home.** This is the default tab to open or create a new presentation in PowerPoint. From here, you can add and duplicate slides as well as cut, copy, and paste text and objects. The Home tab is also where you will select fonts, change font sizes, create bulleted and numbered lists, align text, and order and group objects.

➤ **Insert.** In addition to adding new slides, you can insert tables, images, and charts using the tools on this tab. You will also select Insert if you want to work with shapes, icons, or SmartArt. The Insert tab is shown earlier in this chapter.

➤ **Design.** Apply a preset theme (a collection of fonts, colors and effects) to your presentation slides. You can also change your slide size and format the background using tools on the Design tab.

➤ **Transitions.** If you want to add interesting animations between slides—such as one slide fading away as the next slide is revealed—you will do it with the tools on the Transitions tab. You will also go here if you want to adjust the timing between slides when the presentation is played.

➤ **Animations.** Using the tools on the Animation tab, you can animate individual elements within each PowerPoint slide. The tools located here can also adjust the timing on animations and reorder animations.

➤ **Slide Show.** This is the place to go to start your presentation and display it online. You can also activate *Presenter View*, which will display notes, timers, and a preview of the next slide if you are using a second screen.

➤ **Review.** If you are a careful wordsmith, or work on a team, you will frequently access the Review tab. This is where you will find Power-Point's proofing, layout, and comment tools.

➤ **View.** Whether you want to change your presentation view or access master views, work with the ruler, guides or gridlines, zoom in or out, or quickly change a color presentation to black and white, you will do it all on the View tab.

➤ **Contextual tabs.** PowerPoint has several hidden tabs that pop into view when you are working with certain tools. For instance, when you insert a table into a slide, two special contextual tabs will appear above the Ribbon, containing tools to edit the table's design and layout. There are a number of contextual tabs, some of which will be covered in the chapters that follow.

Unlike previous releases of PowerPoint, the Ribbon and tabs have nearly identical features on both the Windows and Mac versions of PowerPoint 2016.

PowerPoint Online has a Ribbon interface, but it is a bit simpler. For example, it lacks the Slide Show tab, and the other tabs have fewer tools than on the desktop version of PowerPoint.

Keep in mind that Microsoft updates PowerPoint Online with new tools from time to time. Even if a particular feature is missing now, it may be introduced at some point in the future.

Other features of the Ribbon

In addition to the primary tabs summarized above, the Ribbon includes several additional features:

➤ **Tell Me.** New to the Windows version of PowerPoint 2016 and PowerPoint Online is the *Tell Me* feature. It's a small search field located above the Ribbon's toolbar. Type in some text (for instance, "export presentation" or "change slide size") and PowerPoint will display a menu of helpful options. This can save you loads of time you would otherwise have spent scrolling through the Office Help Center. It's useful when you forget where to find a specific tool or you need to know which tool is necessary for a particular task.

➤ **Share.** Look for the silhouette icon on the right side of the Ribbon to display sharing options, which include sharing via OneDrive or sending your presentation as an email attachment. Chapter 4 describes sharing in a bit more detail.

➤ **Quick Access Toolbar.** At the very top left of the Ribbon is the Quick Access Toolbar. Customize it by clicking on the small downward-pointing arrow and checking the tools you use most often. I have configured my Quick Access Toolbar with the icons for Save, Undo, and Repeat. However, you can also add commands such as New, Open, Email, Quick Print, Spelling, and more.

➤ **File Name.** The presentation's file name is located above the Ribbon.

➤ **Your Name.** If you are signed into your Microsoft account, your name will appear in the upper right corner of the Ribbon (Windows and PowerPoint Online; on a Mac, the account info will be displayed in the Backstage View).

➤ **Hiding the Ribbon.** Personally, I prefer to display the entire Ribbon, including the toolbars associated with the active tab. Doing so helps me remember the various options I have for creating and formatting slides. However, it is possible to hide the Ribbon if you find it distracting. Just click on the small arrow icon located to the far right of the Ribbon. You can also use keyboard shortcuts (see Appendix) to show or hide the Ribbon.

The PowerPoint mobile apps for Android and iOS don't use Ribbons, but do have labeled tabs such as Home, Insert, Design, and Animations. On larger devices such as the iPad, the labels will be visible at the top of the screen, but for smaller devices, tap the More Options icon (three dots) to display them. Selecting a tab reveals a limited set of options to apply to the active slide.

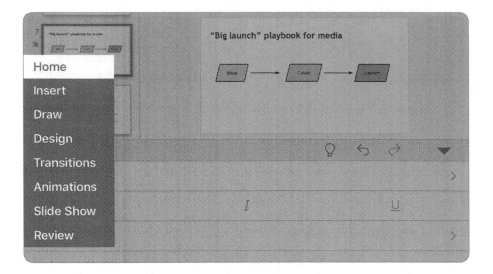

Display options when working on presentations

PowerPoint 2016's View tab includes five Presentation View options and three Master View options. Some are likely to be more useful to novice PowerPoint users than others. I suggest initially familiarizing yourself with the following options:

➤ **Normal.** As PowerPoint's default view for good reason, Normal is the one you'll use most often. It is divided into three sections: the Slide Area, or right three-quarters of the screen; the Slides pane, or left one-quarter of the screen; and finally, the Notes pane, at the bottom of the screen.

➤ You will create and edit slides in the **Slide Area**, scroll through and choose slides in your presentation in the **Slides pane**, and add any necessary notes in the **Notes pane**. You can hide or reveal the Notes pane by clicking the Notes icon in the Status Bar at the bottom of your screen.

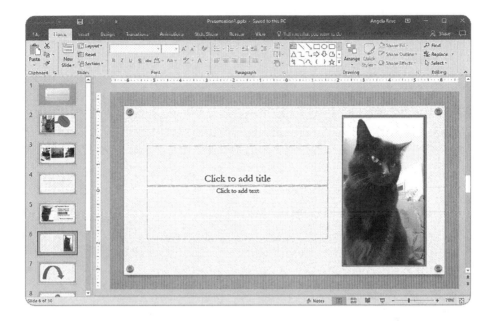

➤ **Reading View.** If you'd like to view your slides in full-screen mode, this option will allow you to do so. You can quickly move through the slides in your presentation using the left and right arrow keys on your keyboard or arrow icons in the Status Bar. Return to the Normal view by clicking the final slide to exit, clicking Esc, or by clicking the Normal icon in the Status Bar.

➤ **Slide Master.** Master slides—if you choose to use them—can control the appearance of your entire presentation, from colors and fonts to shapes, images, and just about everything else. When you edit master slides in Slide Master view, the modifications you make influence the rest of the slides within your presentation. We'll talk more about master slides in Chapter 2.

➤ **Slide Sorter.** Quickly drag slides to reorder your presentation. You can copy, duplicate and delete slides in this view as well.

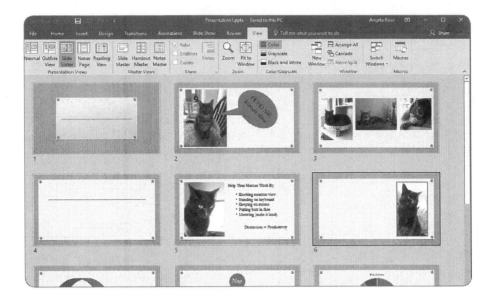

There are two additional essential view options accessible from other tabs on the Ribbon. These are:

> **Slide Show.** Click *From Beginning* or *From Current Slide* on the Slide-show tab, and PowerPoint will play your presentation in full-screen mode according to your preference. You can use Slide Show view to preview your presentation or to actually present it to an audience. Exit Slide Show view by pressing the *Esc* key on your keyboard.

> **Presenter.** If you're presenting your PowerPoint slide deck to an audience in a situation in which you have two displays to work with—such as your laptop and a projector—select *Use Presenter View*. It will display the actual slides on the projector (in Slide Show view), while displaying your presentation in Presenter View on your laptop. This enables you to use a variety of tools to enhance the presentation as it is playing. We will discuss these tools a bit more in Chapter 4.

The default slide size is Widescreen, which has a 16:9 aspect ratio. This is ideal for presenting your PowerPoint deck on widescreen monitors and projectors. However, if you intend to play your presentation on a smaller screen, you can change the slide size to Standard, which has a 4:3 aspect ratio, by selecting the Slide Size tool on the Design tab. Other sizes are available, but these are the two you are most likely to use. When in doubt, stick with widescreen, as it's easier to reduce the size of slides after the fact than to enlarge them.

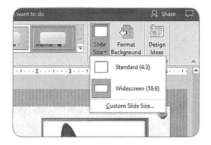

Saving your presentation

Earlier, you learned how to open an existing presentation file, create a new presentation based on a template, or start one from scratch. Once you have started working on that presentation, you are going to want to save the file quickly and as often as you can. No one wants to spend valuable time recreating a file in the event of a computer crash, software malfunction, or power outage caused by acts of nature . . . or cat. My cats love to flop around under my desk. Sometimes they do so vigorously enough to unplug things. Like my computer. But I digress . . .

Saving your PowerPoint file is easy. In PowerPoint Online, saving takes place automatically. For the mobile apps for Android and iOS, files are automatically saved. If you're working with PowerPoint on your desktop, simply click the disk icon in the top left corner of the screen. You can then name the file, select a format, and choose a location to store your presentation—typically OneDrive or your local hard drive.

After giving the file a name and a storage location, saving your progress will be nearly invisible. Use one of the following methods to regularly save an existing presentation:

➤ Click the disk icon.

➤ Select *File > Save.*

➤ Use a keyboard shortcut (Control-S for Windows, Command-S for Macs).

Protip: You can further protect yourself against lost documents by enabling PowerPoint's auto recovery feature. If there is an unexpected system failure, you will be able to access the most recent version of the lost file. In PowerPoint 2016 for Windows, select *File > Options > Save* and then check the boxes next to *Save AutoRecover information,* and *Keep the last AutoRecovered version if I close without saving.* In Power-Point 2016 for Macs, select *Word > Preferences > Save,* and check *Save AutoRecover Info.*

If you want to save a duplicate version of your PowerPoint, it's equally easy to do so. Just select *File > Save As* and enter a new file name. Then select the file format and location in which you wish to save it.

If you use the mobile apps for Android and iOS to create a new presentation, you will be prompted to save a copy to OneDrive or the device when you tap the back arrow or the menu icon (three stacked lines) to leave the presentation. To save a copy, look for an icon with three dots to see what save and export options are available.

Cancel	Save As	Save
Name: lean media 2018		
	Places	
OneDrive - Personal ianlamont@yahoo.com		>
OTHER LOCATIONS		
📱 iPhone		>
••• More		
+ Add a Place		

Which file format should I use?

PowerPoint 2016 includes 28 different file formats, but it's unlikely you'll ever need more than a few of them. The ones you are most likely to use are:

➤ **PowerPoint Presentation (*.pptx).** This is the default save option for all versions of PowerPoint released in the past 10 years. It's also your only save option if you are using PowerPoint Online or the PowerPoint mobile apps (however, it may be possible to export the file as a PDF).

➤ **PowerPoint 97-2003 Presentation (*.ppt).** If you need to collaborate with others who are using an older version of PowerPoint, use this file format.

➤ **PDF (*.pdf).** Saving your presentation in this file format will convert it to an Adobe PDF file. PDFs cannot be played or edited like normal PowerPoint presentations. However, they are great for printing and sharing with people who do not have access to PowerPoint software. In addition, if you don't want the recipient to make changes to the presentation, PDFs are a safe bet.

➤ **PowerPoint Template (*.potx).** When you save your PowerPoint in this file format, it is converted to a template you can use for future presentations. We will dig a little deeper into templates in Chapter 2.

➤ **WMV.** Windows Media Video files can be played on the Web or with a media player. Mac users can save these as .mp4 or .mov files, which can be opened in QuickTime Player.

➤ **JPEG File Interchange Format (*.jpg).** Use the .jpg option if you want to turn your presentation into a collection of graphic files suitable for the Web. If you want to print the files, the .tif format may be a better choice. You can open both JPEG and TIF files in image processing programs such as Photoshop.

Shutting down

Whether you need to move on to your next task or are shutting down for the day, you will want to close out of any open PowerPoint presentation files first. Use one of the following methods:

➤ Click the "X" in the upper right corner of the open file (Windows) or the red dot in the upper left corner (macOS).

➤ Select *File > Close.*

➤ Use a keyboard shortcut: Control-W (Windows) or Command-W (macOS).

Be sure to save the presentation before closing. PowerPoint may display a pop-up prompting you to save the newest version.

For PowerPoint Online, simply shut your browser window or select *Sign Out.* The file will be automatically saved to OneDrive. If you are using one of the PowerPoint mobile apps, simply close the app.

Locating a recovered file

We all get ahead of ourselves from time to time. If you find that you have shut down your PC or mobile device without saving an open PowerPoint file, all is not lost. PowerPoint may be able to recover the unsaved version of your presentation. Sometimes it will automatically open the recovered file when you relaunch PowerPoint. If you don't see it then, you may still be able to find it using the following methods:

➤ In Windows, launch PowerPoint and choose *Open Other Presentations* from the Start Screen. Scroll to the bottom of the list of recent presentations and select *Recover Unsaved Presentations.* PowerPoint will search your computer for any available unsaved files.

➤ If you are using a Mac, select *Recent* in Backstage View and see if the list contains the recovered file.

CHAPTER 2

Creating a basic presentation

At its simplest, a PowerPoint presentation is merely a collection of slides, each one containing text and images or other graphics. However, for something so straightforward, PowerPoint presentations have the potential to go horribly wrong.

Take, for instance, a recent story that made headlines in outlets as varied as *Fox News*, *Daily Mail,* and *Mashable.* A young British man was setting up a date with another gentleman he had met online. In response to the question, "Where should we go?" he decided to create a PowerPoint presentation for an audience of one. It contained everything from goofy pictures to a summary slide.

In Conclusion

- The aforementioned options are just that, options. If you just want to go for a drink at a pub I am okay with that too – but I thought it would be nice to suggest something more fun and fulfilling.
- If you have any suggestions I am willing to consider them too

- I look forward to hearing back from you soon.
- x

His six-slide deck was a textbook example of common PowerPoint mistakes, including full sentences, jumbled font styles, extra line breaks, and low-quality images downloaded from the Internet. His potential sweetheart blocked him on social media, and the young man found himself back in the icy waters of loneliness.

It's too bad he didn't take the time to learn some PowerPoint best practices first, right? Fortunately for you, the basics are right here at your fingertips.

> **Protip:** Plan your presentation before you even open PowerPoint. It shouldn't be a rambling regurgitation of your every thought. Rather, it should contain concise, targeted messages. Drafting an outline is often very helpful. And don't fail to consider the time your audience has available. Some experts recommend limiting yourself to 15 slides for a 30-minute presentation. That's two minutes per slide.

Inserting and editing new slides

Whether you click on *New Slide* on the Home tab or *New Slide* on the Insert tab, PowerPoint will give you the option to start with a totally blank slide or choose one that already contains placeholders for text and images arranged in various layouts.

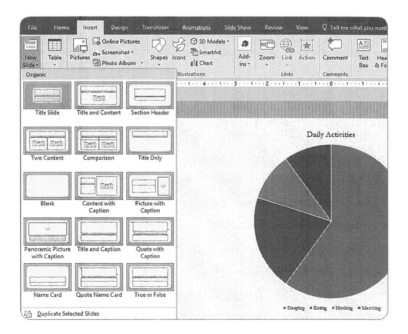

Slide layouts and themes

PowerPoint 2016's default theme is *Office*, which has nine predesigned layouts ranging from *Title Slide* and *Section Header* to *Content with Caption* and *Picture with Caption*. Simply click on the layout you want to use, and PowerPoint will insert a slide with that layout into the presentation (if you are choosing a layout after clicking on *New Slide*), or change the current slide to that layout (if you are choosing a layout after clicking on *Layout* on the Home tab).

If PowerPoint's Office theme and associated layouts do not thrill you, choosing a new theme is simple. You'll find 34 prebuilt themes on the Design tab, with each one available in multiple variants. Hover your mouse over a theme or variant to preview it on your slide. You can also select themes using the PowerPoint apps for Android and iOS.

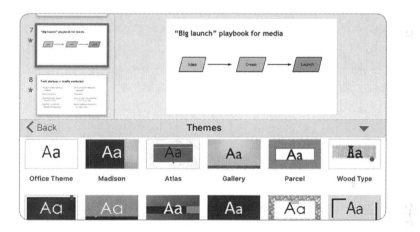

The layouts available for each slide vary depending on the PowerPoint theme you use. For example, while the *Office* theme includes nine layouts, the *Facet* theme includes 14 prebuilt layouts.

Customizing slide layouts

While prebuilt layouts can give you a head start on slide design, you may find that their placeholders don't always satisfy your needs. For example, you may want to move the text and photo boxes around, resize them, or even add additional elements. It's all possible—and probably easier than you imagine.

Adjusting placeholders

Before you can adjust a text, picture or content placeholder, you'll need to select it by hovering your mouse over it and clicking. You will know you are successful when the placeholder's outline changes from a dashed to a solid line. Now you can perform the following actions:

➤ **Move.** Simply click the placeholder again and drag it to a new location on the slide.

➤ **Resize.** Click and drag a corner or side until the placeholder is as large or small as you desire.

➤ **Rotate.** Click the rotation handle at the top of the placeholder and then drag it to the left or right.

➤ **Delete.** Press the *Backspace* key on your keyboard.

Once you have your placeholders where you want them, you can type text into the text boxes and place images in the picture and content boxes. Simply click and type or—in the case of images and other content—click the icon and follow the prompts.

The mobile apps for Android and iOS also allow placeholders to be moved, resized, and rotated. However, instead of using a mouse, you use your finger to manipulate the objects on the screen. Double-tap placeholders to add text.

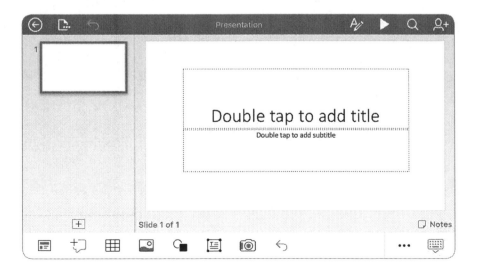

Adding text boxes

If you want to place additional text elements on your slide that are not included in the layout, you'll need to add one or more text boxes. There are two simple ways to do so:

➤ If you are on the Home tab, you can select the Text Box icon within the library of Drawing Tools. Then position your mouse over the slide, and click and drag the text box until it's the size you need.

➤ If you are on the Insert tab, just select the Text Box tool before positioning your mouse over the slide, clicking and dragging the text box until it's the size you need.

You can move, resize, rotate or delete the text boxes you create in exactly the same way as described for placeholders.

Protip: Don't get carried away with adding or expanding slide elements. Text boxes are easy to add, but too many will yield a text-heavy presentation that can turn off prospective audiences. The text you use should highlight your main points and emphasize facts, statistics, and other snippets of information. In most cases, you'll want to avoid paragraphs and to stick to sentence fragments. For best results, your slides should be a visual aid for your audience, not a transcript of your verbal presentation. The example below shows the difference between the two.

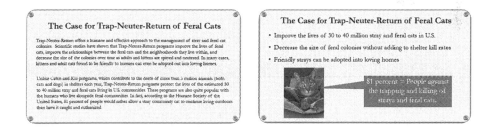

Formatting slide backgrounds

PowerPoint's default theme, Office, defaults to a white slide background. Many of the program's other prebuilt themes do as well, though there are also visually complex themes that have multicolored designs or graphic elements in the background.

Regardless of the theme you choose to use, it's easy to change the background style on one or more of your slides. Do so by accessing the Design tab and selecting the *Format Background* tool.

When you click the *Format Background* tool, the Format Background pane will appear. The options displayed depend on the background of the current theme. For example, the default Office theme uses a solid fill background. You can change the color and transparency of that fill using the *Color* or *Transparency* tools within the Format Background pane.

More complex themes may utilize gradients, pictures, textures, or patterns in their backgrounds. You can change the background elements used on any slide from the Format Background pane. Simply select the fill option you desire and use the displayed tools to make adjustments. If you want those changes reflected on every slide in your presentation, click *Apply to All*.

Don't hesitate to play around with the tools in the Format Background pane to learn how they work and see how adjustments affect your slides. If you don't like the results, you can click *Reset Background* to return to the preset background fill for your chosen theme.

> **Protip:** When it comes to backgrounds, simpler is generally better—especially if you're a new PowerPoint user. Clunky use of pictures, textures, and fills can negatively affect the readability of your slide text. Additionally, consider where you'll be presenting your PowerPoint deck when choosing your background fill. In dark rooms, darker backgrounds with lighter text may be more readable. However, in brighter rooms, a lighter background with darker text may yield better results.

Using master slides

While working with master slides is more suited to intermediate PowerPoint users than to beginners, I felt it was important to touch on them here. The Slide Master feature is an easy way to add and adjust common elements—those you want to appear on every slide in your presentation—in one place.

For example, if you are working on a corporate presentation and want to include your company logo on every slide, you can add it using the Slide Master and save yourself the hassle of manually inserting the logo into each one.

To reveal the Slide Master tab, simply click the *Slide Master* button on the View tab. The master slide is the top slide in the Slide pane on the left of the screen. Layouts related to the master slide will appear below it. You can move, add, or delete elements on the master slide or associated layouts, and all of your slides that follow that master will change accordingly. You can also make text style changes including font, font size, alignment, color, and more.

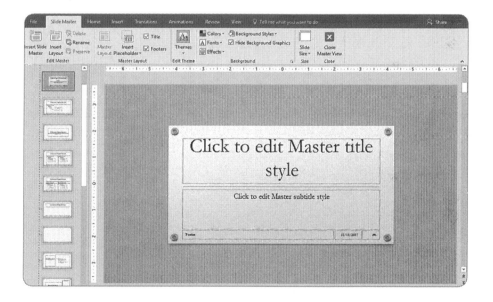

To return to Normal view, select *Close Master View* on the Slide Master tab or click the Normal View icon in the Status Bar at the bottom of your screen.

As of this writing, the Slide Master tab cannot be accessed in PowerPoint Online or the PowerPoint mobile apps.

Slide order within your presentation

If you've taken the time to create a written outline before beginning your presentation design, you likely already have a solid idea of the order in which your slides should appear. However, should you change your mind, it's simple to move, delete, and even duplicate single or multiple slides.

How to move a slide

PowerPoint will arrange your slides in the Slide pane on the left side of the screen in the order they were created. Should you decide to change that order, you can do so using one of these methods:

➤ While in *Normal* view (*View > Normal*) use your pointer to "grab" the thumbnail of the slide you want to move in the Slide pane and drag it to a new location.

➤ While in *Slide Sorter* view (*View > Slide Sorter*), grab the thumbnail of the slide you want to move and drag it to the new location.

Regardless of the method you choose, you can move multiple slides by pressing and holding the *Ctrl* key (*Command* for Mac) on your keyboard, selecting each slide you want to move, and then dragging them all at once to the new location.

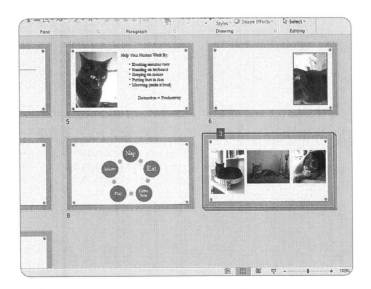

The same methods can be used for PowerPoint Online. In the mobile version, use your finger to drag and rearrange slides (flip your phone to Landscape View if you don't see the slides on the left side of the screen).

How to delete a slide

Perhaps you accidentally created two slides with the same text and need to remove the duplicate or are trying to make your presentation shorter by eliminating all but the most essential slides. You can delete those you no longer want using the following methods:

➤ While in *Normal* view (*View > Normal*), right-click on the thumbnail of the slide you want to delete in the Slide pane. You can then click *Delete Slide*.

➤ While in *Slide Sorter* view (*View > Slide Sorter*), right-click on the thumbnail of the slide you want to delete and then click *Delete Slide*.

➤ In either view, select the slide and press the *delete* or *backspace* button on your keyboard (this method also works for PowerPoint Online).

Select multiple slides for deletion by pressing and holding the *Ctrl* key on your keyboard as you select the slides. Then, press the *delete* or *backspace* button on your keyboard or right-click and select *Delete Slide*.

For the Android or iOS versions of PowerPoint, a light, quick tap on a slide should reveal a menu of options, including one to delete the slide.

How to duplicate a slide

Duplicating a slide is just as easy as deleting one. In *Normal* or *Slide Sorter* view, right-click over the slide you wish to duplicate and select *Duplicate Slide*. On the Home and Insert tabs, you can also use the *New Slide* drop-down menu and select *Duplicate Selected Slides* at the bottom of the menu.

This tool is extremely handy if you create a slide with a design and layout that you love and wish to reuse throughout the presentation. Just duplicate the slide(s) and swap out text and images as needed.

Formatting text

If you are familiar with other programs in the Microsoft Office suite (including Microsoft Word), then you probably already know most of what you need to format text in PowerPoint. The font and paragraph tools on the Home tab offer the most straightforward means of formatting text—simply highlight the text within a selected text box and use one of the buttons or menus to change its appearance. These tools include:

➤ **Font and Font Size.** PowerPoint offers a number of built-in fonts, ranging from the classic to the creative. When scrolling through the options, the top of the list will show the fonts used within the current theme. Select any other font from the *All Fonts* list, if you prefer. In addition to picking a font, you can also select the size (for instance, 28-point Calibri).

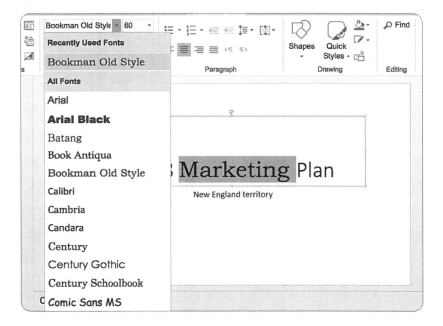

➤ **Bold, Italic, Underline, and Text Shadow.** The first three do exactly what you expect them to. Many people also use the relevant shortcut keys—*Ctrl+B*, *Ctrl+I*, and *Ctrl+U*. The *Text Shadow* button applies a slightly offset shadow that gives selected text a 3D feel.

➤ **Character Spacing.** Adjust the spacing between characters from *Very Tight* to *Very Loose*. *Normal* spacing is the default option, but slightly looser spacing can sometimes improve readability depending on the font you have chosen to use.

➤ **Font Color.** Change the color of your text to almost any shade you can imagine. Note that certain colors may reduce readability.

➤ **Bullets and Numbering.** Use these tools to create bulleted or numbered lists. Various style options are offered for each type of list.

➤ **Alignment.** Default is *Align Left* for most themes, but you can also select *Align Right*, *Center*, or *Justify*.

➤ **Line Spacing.** Use this tool to adjust the space between lines of text within a text box. Increasing the space between lines can improve the readability of some fonts.

➤ **Text Direction.** Let's say you have a text box stretching from the top to the bottom of the left side of a slide and want to rotate the text within it so it reads bottom to top. You can do that with this tool.

➤ **Align Text.** Use this tool to align your text within a text box's vertical space. Choose from *Top*, *Middle* or *Bottom*.

You can use these tools before you begin typing in a text box or after the fact by highlighting the text and then choosing the relevant tools. Note that PowerPoint's ruler may come in handy when you want to adjust the spacing between characters, lines, or bullet points, or make sure your indentations are aligned. To display the ruler, simply check the box next to the *Ruler* tool on the View tab. You also have the option to display *Gridlines* and *Guides*. To hide any of these tools, just uncheck their boxes on the View tab.

It is possible to make changes to the fonts used throughout your presentation by altering them within your PowerPoint's theme or on the Master slide. However, those methods are better suited to intermediate PowerPoint users, so we will not cover them here. If you want to learn more, type *Change the fonts in a presentation* into the *Tell Me* field and select *Get help on . . .* for a list of related Help tutorials.

PowerPoint Online and the mobile apps for Android and iOS have many of the same formatting tools, but not all of them. The options for a specific tool may also be more limited than what's available in the desktop version of PowerPoint. For instance, the font and color options in PowerPoint Online are restricted to a smaller set.

Protip: Readability is key when creating PowerPoint slides. If your text isn't readable, it won't be effective, as shown in the sample below. If you elect to stray from the fonts built into PowerPoint's themes, experts recommend keeping your fonts simple and choosing *sans serif* typefaces such as Calibri, Arial, Helvetica, or Gill Sans. Additionally, font size is important. If you're presenting your PowerPoint on a screen in a large room, you'll want to scale text larger than you would if it were to be viewed by someone on a laptop. Finally, avoid cluttering your presentation with too many font styles. One style for headlines and a second style for body text is a safe bet.

Images

Images and PowerPoint go together quite naturally. In fact, effective use of visuals can reduce your reliance on text to emphasize the main points of your presentation. As with most other basics, PowerPoint has made working with image files very simple. (And don't worry: for those of you who want to insert some cat videos or other clips into your presentations, I'll cover video and audio in the next chapter.)

How to insert an image

While it's possible to add images to multiple slides using the *Slide Master* tool, or into the background using the *Format Background* tool, we're going to limit our focus to taking image files stored on your computer or downloaded from the Internet and inserting them into a single slide.

➤ If you want to insert an image that is saved on your computer, select the *Pictures* tool on the Insert tab. When the dialog box opens, navigate to the image file that you want to insert. Select the file, and then click *Insert*. PowerPoint will drop the image onto your slide and display the Picture Tools Format tab on the Ribbon.

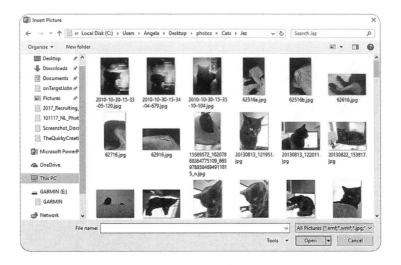

➤ If the image you wish to use is available on the Internet, start by selecting the *Online Pictures* tool on the Insert tab. A dialog box will open, prompting you to retrieve an image you have saved to OneDrive or search the Internet for a suitable image. Unless you have permission from an artist to use an image—be it a photo, illustration, or diagram—it's safest to select from those that are tagged *Creative Commons*. Click *Insert* and PowerPoint will drop the image onto your slide and simultaneously reveal the Picture Tools Format tab to perform additional formatting tasks.

In PowerPoint Online, image choices are limited to what's stored on your computer's hard drive. PowerPoint for Android and iOS allow you to insert images from the device's photo application or from the camera.

How to move, resize or rotate an image

You will move, resize, and rotate images using the same methods you used for placeholders and text boxes. Begin by hovering your mouse over the image you want to work with and clicking it. When the outline changes from a dashed line to a solid line, you can then perform the following actions upon the image:

➤ **Move.** "Grab" the image with your pointer and drag it to a new location on the slide.

➤ **Resize.** Click and drag a corner or side until the image is as large or small as you desire.

➤ **Rotate.** Click the rotation handle at the top of the image and then drag it to the left or right.

➤ **Delete.** Press the *Backspace* key on your keyboard.

Basic image edits

The number of edits you can make to an image within PowerPoint is astonishing. There are tools for everything from removing backgrounds and adjusting brightness and contrast to adding artistic effects. Because this book is primarily for beginners and others who want a quick refresher, I'm only going to outline the basics that can be found on the Picture Tools Format tab in the desktop version of PowerPoint. These include:

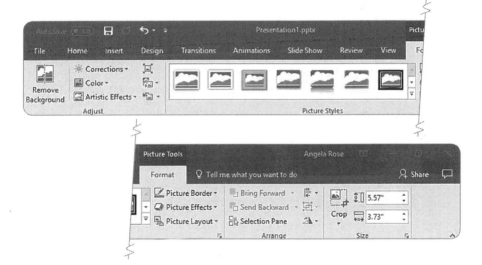

➤ **Compress Pictures.** If you've inserted a lot of high-resolution images into your presentation, it may have reached a cumbersome size that makes it hard to transfer, share, or sync. You can use this tool to compress images, which can reduce the PowerPoint file size by 25% or more. This is very helpful if you intend to email the PowerPoint to someone or want to be able to play it online. Smaller file sizes are easier to send, and load more quickly, too.

➤ **Change Picture.** Don't like the image you've selected, but want to keep the placement and size? Use this tool to pop a replacement image into the slide.

➤ **Picture Border.** Add and remove outlines and adjust color and weight.

➤ **Picture Effects.** You can add shadows, glow, beveled edges, and more.

➤ **Picture Styles.** If you love borders and effects, choosing from the gallery of image styles is the quickest way to apply them to an image on your slide. Hover your mouse over each one to preview the results.

Protip: Remember that cheesy Microsoft clip art from the 80s and 90s? It's still out there on the Internet, or maybe stored on your company's network. Avoid using it. High-quality stock photography is a much better choice if you want to create an impressive presentation. When choosing stock photography, think about what the images say to your audience and how that communicates your message. Shutterstock.com offers millions of royalty-free stock images that can be licensed for a small fee.

Aligning and grouping objects

Much like my couch (or my bed, depending on which one I want to use), PowerPoint slides usually contain more than one cat—or object, in the case of slides. Objects can include multiple text boxes, or an arrangement of text boxes, images, charts, graphs, and SmartArt Graphics (super-cool infographics we'll discuss further in the next chapter). You don't want to simply jumble the objects on the page. The more complex your slide, the more visually pleasing it will be to align and group the objects upon it.

How to align objects

In the desktop version of PowerPoint, dashed orange lines and arrows appear around objects when you move them in PowerPoint. These are the software's alignment and spacing guides. While you can use them to align the objects on your slide, getting it perfect can be frustratingly tricky. Instead, I suggest using one of the following methods to quickly complete the task:

➤ While holding down the *Shift* key on your keyboard, click on the objects you want to align. This will reveal the Picture Tools Format tab. Select *Align* and then choose *Align Selected Objects*. Select the *Align* tool again and then choose one of the available alignment options. The objects will align accordingly.

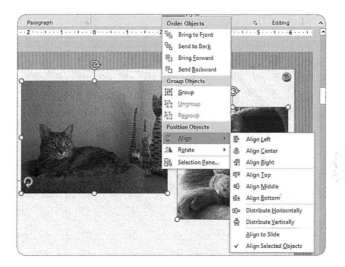

➤ If you want to align one or more objects to a specific location on the slide, you will choose *Align to Slide* from the *Align* tool drop-down before selecting one of the other available alignment options. Remember to hold down the *Shift* key to select multiple objects.

➤ You can also use the *Distribute Vertically* and *Distribute Horizontally* options under *Align* tool to arrange the objects an equal distance from one another.

How to group objects

Grouping—or attaching—multiple objects together makes it easier to move them around your slide without changing their distance from one another. Grouping also allows users to uniformly increase or decrease the size of the attached objects.

Let's say you have three separate images of cats aligned horizontally across your slide and you want to move the entire clowder (that's right, a clowder is a group of cats) up a bit. Follow these steps:

➤ Hold down the *Shift* key on your keyboard as you click each of the three images.

➤ Next, click the *Group* tool on the Picture Tools Format tab.

➤ Select *Group* and then drag that clowder to the new location.

➤ If you later want to ungroup your cats—or other objects—simply click the Group tool again and select *Ungroup*.

As of this writing, grouping objects is not supported in PowerPoint Online or the mobile apps for Android and iOS.

How to order objects

If two or more objects on a slide overlap, you will need to reorder them if you want to adjust which object appears in the front or the back. To do this in the desktop version of PowerPoint, click the object you want to change before selecting the *Bring Forward* or *Send Backward* tool on the Picture Tools Format tab. This will change that object's order by one level.

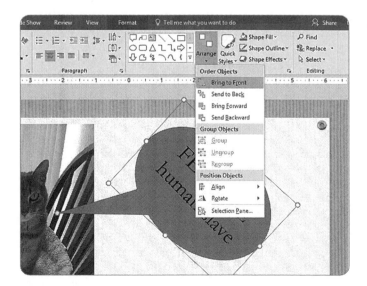

If you want to send an object all the way to the back or bring it all the way to the front, simply choose the appropriate option from the drop-down under the *Bring Forward* or *Send Backward* tool.

In PowerPoint Online, select *Arrange* on the Home tab to order objects.

This functionality is not yet supported in the PowerPoint mobile apps.

> **Protip:** If your slide has a lot of overlapping objects, you may find it difficult to select the individual object you are after. In that case, the *Selection Pane* tool on the Picture Tools Format tab can really simplify the process. Just click on it and then choose the object or objects you want to align, group or order from the list that is displayed.

How to zoom

Sometimes you may find that you want to take a closer look at the objects within the slides you are designing. On both the desktop and online versions of PowerPoint, you can zoom in or out on your presentation using the *Zoom* tool on the View tab or the *Zoom* toggle on the Status Bar at the bottom of your screen.

CHAPTER 3

Intermediate features

If you want to create a presentation that is visually interesting for your audience, you don't have to rely on text formatting and images alone. PowerPoint has tools for adding charts, tables, shapes, infographics, video, and audio to enhance your message, along with animations and transitions to draw emphasis to important details. While some of these tools have lots of options, the basic use of each is within the reach of even beginner PowerPoint users.

Protip: With so many nifty PowerPoint features at your disposal, it's all too easy to get carried away and wind up with slides that are cluttered at best and incomprehensible at worst. Remember to leave white space—or empty space between objects—in all of your slides. You don't need to fill every inch with shapes, images, and other graphics to create an engaging and effective presentation.

Shapes and SmartArt

Many of PowerPoint's pre-designed templates and themes use shapes to create visual interest in their designs. The *Badge* Theme, for example, prominently features circles, bars and wavy lines within the various slide layouts it offers. However, you can also customize individual slides with shapes that you choose. The software has made it simple to insert basic ovals, rectangles, and lines as well as complex infographics (known as SmartArt Graphics) into your slide designs.

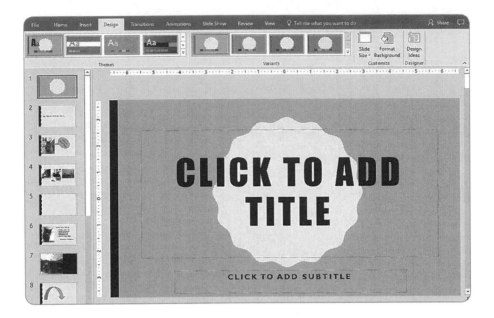

How to insert simple shapes

You'll find shape tools in several locations within PowerPoint's tabs. On the Home tab, you can insert a shape by selecting one from the Shape Gallery in both the desktop version of PowerPoint (Windows/macOS) as well as in PowerPoint Online. You can also access an expanded Shape Gallery using the *Shapes* tool on the Insert tab. In PowerPoint for Android and iOS, the Shapes tool can be accessed via the Insert tab.

Simply select the shape you want and then click the slide in the location you wish it to appear. From there you can:

➤ **Resize the shape** by clicking and dragging its sizing handles.

➤ **Move the shape** by clicking within it and dragging it to a new location.

➤ **Rotate the shape** by clicking the rotation handle above the shape and then dragging it left or right.

➤ **Delete the shape** by clicking within it and then pressing the Backspace key on your keyboard.

Simple shape edits

PowerPoint also provides tools to edit any shape you've already inserted. You can quickly change the Shape Fill, Shape Outline, and add Shape Effects using the tools on the Home tab. For even more options, navigate to the Drawing Tools Format tab where you can:

➤ **Edit Shape.** Use this tool to change the shape to an entirely different selection in the Shape Gallery or adjust individual points to create a freeform result.

➤ **Shape Styles.** Quickly change your shape fill, border, and effects to a variety of preset combinations within your PowerPoint theme. Hover over each one to see a preview of the results.

➤ **Shape Fill.** Choose a new fill color, add a gradient or texture, or fill the shape with a picture.

➤ **Shape Effects.** Add shadow or glow, bevel the shape's edges, and more.

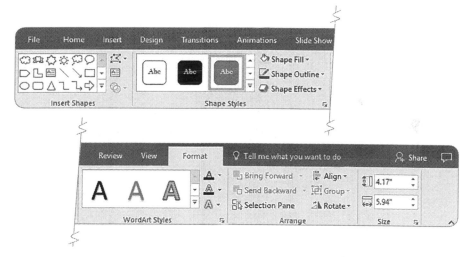

How to insert SmartArt Graphics

SmartArt Graphics, also known as infographics outside of PowerPoint, are graphic representations of data designed to communicate information quickly, clearly, and concisely. While you could hire a professional graphic artist to create custom infographics for you using a program such as Adobe Illustrator, the desktop and online versions of PowerPoint can handle the basics.

To get started, click the *SmartArt* tool on the Insert tab. A pop-up window will appear, which contains the SmartArt Gallery. As you browse the gallery, clicking on a selection will yield an explanation of possible uses. Select the graphic you want to insert, click *OK* on the dialog box, and PowerPoint will add the SmartArt to your slide.

From there you can resize, move, rotate, and delete the SmartArt using the same methods you use to make such changes to images and simple shapes (refer to Chapter 2 if you need a refresher).

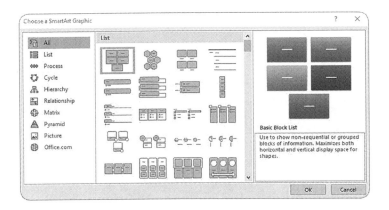

SmartArt Graphic edits

Because SmartArt comprises multiple shapes and text boxes, editing a SmartArt Graphic can get a bit complex. You'll need to add and format text within each placeholder text box. You may also want to adjust one or more of the shapes.

> ➤ **Add text to a placeholder** by clicking within the placeholder. You can then type in your text and format the font, font size, and color exactly as you would with any other text box, using the tools on the Home tab or the Mini Toolbar.

> ➤ **If your graphic contains a lot of text placeholders**, you may find it easier to add text in the Text pane rather than typing it directly into each box. You can reveal the Text pane by clicking on the small white arrow tab on the left of the SmartArt box. You can also format your text within the Text pane, and that formatting will be reflected within the SmartArt Graphic.

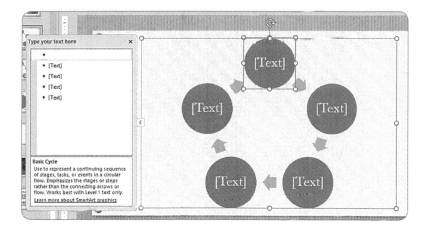

➤ **Change the SmartArt layout** by selecting a new one from the Layout Gallery on the SmartArt Tools Design tab.

➤ **Change SmartArt shape colors as a group** using the Change Colors tool on the SmartArt Tools Design tab.

➤ **Change individual SmartArt shape colors** using the Shape Fill tool on the SmartArt Format tab. You can also change individual shape outlines and apply effects from this tab.

➤ **Change SmartArt styles** by simply selecting another one from the SmartArt Styles gallery on the SmartArt Tools Design tab.

Protip: The SmartArt Gallery contains an extensive variety of SmartArt options ranging from lists to graphics that you can use to illustrate hierarchies, cycles, and relationships. It's tempting to go crazy and add SmartArt everywhere, and customize it as you go. However, you'll spend less time editing SmartArt if you consider the amount of text required before making selections.

Charts

Much like SmartArt Graphics, charts allow you to communicate information graphically. However, while SmartArt Graphics generally work best for communicating an idea with words and graphics, charts are better suited for communicating numerical data. To make data entry easy, the desktop version of PowerPoint even allows you to copy in data from Excel spreadsheets.

How to insert a chart

To add a chart to a PowerPoint slide, select the *Chart* tool on the Insert tab. A pop-up window will display the Chart Gallery. The gallery is organized by type of chart and includes categories such as column, line, and pie charts as well as histogram, waterfall, and funnel charts. Within each category, you'll see multiple options. The data you need to convey will determine the best chart to use.

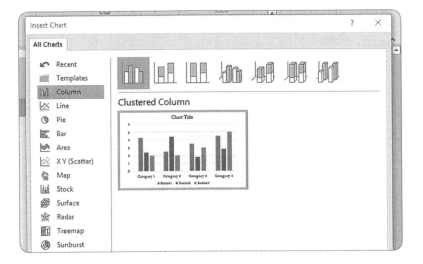

Select the chart you want and then click *OK* within the pop-up window. A miniature spreadsheet—complete with placeholder data—will appear. You will replace that data with your own and it will populate the chart. Entering data is easy. Simply double-click within each cell and type in your new data.

If you have a lot of data to enter, you might find it easier to do this in an actual Excel spreadsheet and then copy and paste it into the PowerPoint spreadsheet pop-up. When you're done, shut the pop-up and your chart will be complete. You can update the data in a chart at any time by selecting the chart and then using the *Edit Data* tool on the Chart Tools Design tab.

If you need to move or resize your chart, you'll do so using the same methods used for pictures, shapes, and SmartArt Graphics (review one of these earlier sections for a refresher if needed).

PowerPoint Online and the PowerPoint app for Android and iOS do not currently allow users to add charts. However, the Insert tab in the online and mobile versions of PowerPoint have an option to add tables that can contain text or numbers.

Protip: While you can add simple tables to a PowerPoint slide, charts offer a more visually appealing way to convey important numerical data. Remember, snippets of data are easier to understand and recall than columns of numbers such as you would generally find in a table.

Changing the appearance of charts

You can quickly change the appearance of a chart using the Quick Layout tool on the Chart Tools Design tab. Options include changing colors (*Chart Colors* tool), altering the style (*Chart Styles* tool) or even swapping in an entirely new chart type (*Change Chart Type* tool).

On the Chart Tools Format tab, you'll find additional tools to modify a chart's fill, outline, and effects. The tools work identically to the ones you've already encountered when modifying shapes and SmartArt Graphics.

Videos

If you want to further enhance your PowerPoint presentation, you have the option to insert video within slides. Smart use of these elements can help you engage your audience and add another dimension to your slide deck. Your video will begin playing immediately when you reach that slide during your presentation.

How to insert a video

Let's say you want to add a hilarious clip of a cat doing taxes to your PowerPoint slide. To do so, you will use the *Video* tool on the Insert tab. You can insert an online video or a video you have stored on your PC. Select the appropriate option and a pop-up window will open. Navigate to the video file storage location (if on your PC) or choose OneDrive or YouTube (if getting a video from the Web). Alternatively, you can paste video embed code if you have copied it from another location.

Once you have located the video you want, click *OK* on the pop-up window. PowerPoint will add the video to your slide. You will resize, move, and delete the video the same way you would a stationary image. Visit that section in the previous chapter for a refresher if necessary.

PowerPoint Online limits video selections to online sources such as You-Tube. The PowerPoint mobile apps for Android and iOS require access to videos stored on the device.

Editing and formatting a video

Using the tools on the Video Tools Format tab, you can make a multitude of adjustments ranging from correcting the brightness and contrast, to choosing a new Video Style, to altering the video's shape and border.

The tools on the Video Tools Playback tab can be used to trim your video, add a fade in or fade out effect, adjust volume, and insert captions. While I'm not going to go into detail on video formatting or editing in this book, you can find great Microsoft tutorials using the Tell Me tool.

Text and object animations

Videos aren't the only way to capture your audience's attention with moving pictures. PowerPoint includes tools you can use to animate text, images, shapes, and other objects. You'll find them on the Animations tab on all versions of PowerPoint.

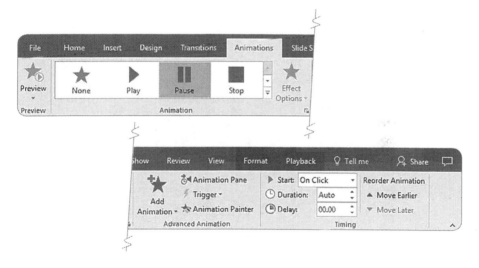

Animation types

Animations come in four basic types: entrance, emphasis, exit, and motion path. Choose one of the following options depending on what you want the animated object to do:

➤ **Entrance animations** control the entry of an object into a slide. For example, if you choose the *Fade* animation, the text or object you apply it to will fade into view. Choose *Zoom* and it will zoom into view from a distant perspective.

➤ **Emphasis animations** can affect an object already on a slide and are triggered by a mouse click. For example, you can apply the *Pulse* animation to a text box to make its contents pulse in place. Use *Bold Reveal* and your text will change to a bold font.

➤ **Exit animations** control the exit of an object from a slide. Choose *Fade* and the text or object will fade from view. Choose *Zoom* and it will zoom away into the distance.

➤ **Motion path animations** allow you to move an object in a predetermined path such as an arc or a loop.

Applying an animation

To apply an animation to a text box, picture or other object, you will first select the object you want to animate on the slide. From there:

➤ Select the animation you wish to use from the Animation Gallery on the Animations tab.

➤ PowerPoint will apply the animation to the object. You'll know the animation has been applied when a small number appears next to it on the slide.

➤ If the animation has additional options, you can access them using the *Effect Options* tool on the Animations tab. The *Fly In* entrance animation, for example, has options that let you specify the direction from which the text or object will enter the slide.

➤ To preview the animation or animations, click the *Preview* tool on the Animations tab (desktop version of PowerPoint), or play the presentation (any version).

➤ If you don't like an animation and want to remove it, simply click the small number next to the object and then press the *Backspace* key on your keyboard.

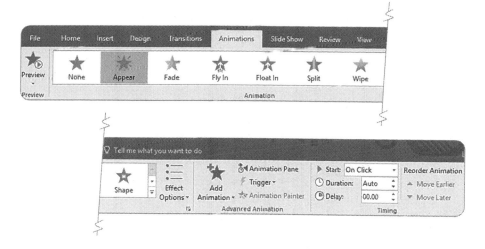

You can adjust when your animation starts and how long it lasts using the *Timing* tools on the Animations tab. If you have multiple animations running on a single slide, you can also reorder them here.

Slide transitions

Transitions are special effects that you can use between slides. For example, one slide might morph or fade into another. Or you might have your next slide push the previous one out of the way. The desktop versions of Power-Point, PowerPoint Online, and the PowerPoint mobile apps include a variety of transitions you can apply, ranging from subtle to dramatic.

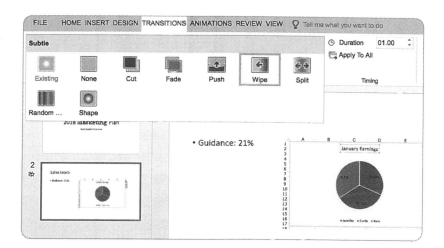

Applying a transition

When applying transitions in PowerPoint for Windows and macOS, you'll work with the slide thumbnails in the Slide Navigation pane on the left side of your screen (in Normal view). Select the slide you want to appear *after* the transition, then:

➤ Choose a transition from the Transition Gallery on the Transitions tab.

➤ PowerPoint will apply the transition to the slide. You'll know the transition has been applied when an asterisk (*) appears next to its thumbnail in the Slide Navigation pane.

➤ If the transition you've selected has additional options, you can access them using the *Effect Options* tool on the Transitions tab. The *Push* transition, for example, includes options to select which direction the previous slide should push from.

➤ You can also adjust the duration of the transition and select sound effects using tools on the Transitions tab.

➤ To preview a transition, just click the *Preview* tool on the Transitions tab.

➤ If you don't like a transition and want to remove it, simply select the slide and then click *None* in the Transition Gallery.

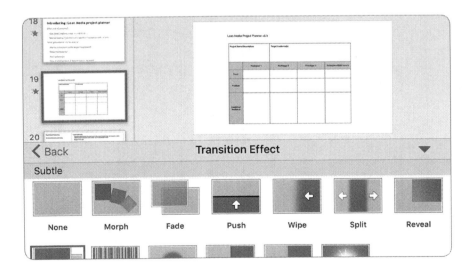

Transitions are also available in PowerPoint Online and the mobile apps for Android and iOS devices, but with fewer customization options than the desktop version of PowerPoint. Visit the Transitions tab to see what's available.

Protip: While it's possible to add transitions between every slide in your presentation, use them sparingly, such as when switching between sections in a longer presentation. The same goes for animations. Too many will only distract your audience. If you can't resist trying them, at least use them smartly, such as when calling attention to key takeaways.

CHAPTER 4

Proofing, printing, and sharing

So far, you've learned how to work with the basic elements of a PowerPoint presentation, and even learned about many of the bells and whistles that can give your slide decks pizzazz while emphasizing the most important points of your message. However, the effectiveness of even the most perfectly designed presentation is going to suffer if your copy includes typos or inaccurate data that could have been eliminated through proofing and collaboration.

Proofing a presentation

As a careful writer who prides herself on producing error-free first drafts, few things are as horrifying as finding a typographical error in my copy *after* I've submitted it to an editor. The horror would be 100 times worse if I were to see that typo projected in 40-point type in front of a room full of people!

Fortunately, catching embarrassing typos, spelling errors, and (to a limited extent) grammatical blunders is as easy in PowerPoint as it is in Microsoft Word (check out one of my other guides, *Microsoft Word In 30 Minutes*, for more information about using Word).

There are two ways to proof the text within your presentation using the desktop version of PowerPoint:

➤ **Automatic.** By default, PowerPoint's proofing function is set to *Check spelling as you type*. Potential misspellings will be underlined in red. Right-click on the underlined word and you can choose to use the suggested correction, ignore it, or add the word as-is to PowerPoint's dictionary.

➤ **Using the *Spelling* tool.** Located on the Review tab, clicking this tool will launch PowerPoint's spell check function and open the Spelling pane, which will be located on the right of your screen. On the Spelling pane, you will find additional options including *Ignore All* and *Change All*. Once you make a decision regarding one potential error, PowerPoint moves on to the next.

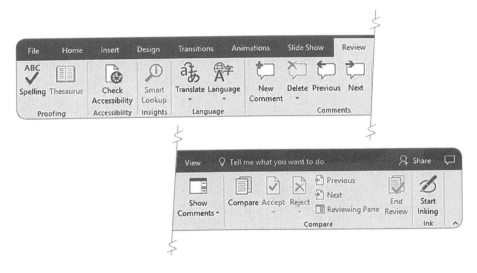

You can also run a grammar check on your PowerPoint presentation. To do so, you'll need to adjust the software's proofing options in *File > Options > Proofing*. Just check the box next to *Check grammar with spelling* and then re-run your spelling check. Potential grammar errors will be underlined in blue.

I personally don't find the grammar check feature very helpful when working with PowerPoint slides. That's because if you're following some of the design recommendations in this book, the copy in your deck will contain lots of sentence fragments and bulleted text—both of which are likely to be flagged as errors by the grammar check feature.

The spelling and proofing tools in the desktop version of PowerPoint are not available in PowerPoint Online or the PowerPoint apps for Android and iOS.

Presentation collaboration tools

PowerPoint presentations are rarely created in a vacuum. Whether you want to gather feedback from coworkers or need a boss or client to sign off on your work, PowerPoint 2016 and PowerPoint Online include helpful tools that make adding, viewing, and replying to comments easy. You will need to be in Normal view (*View > Normal*) to use these tools.

Collaboration

To use PowerPoint's collaboration features, you must first share your document. To do so from any version of PowerPoint, click or tap the Share icon (which looks like a silhouette) in the upper right corner of the PowerPoint interface. If the document is not already stored in the cloud, you will be prompted to save it to OneDrive.

In the desktop version of PowerPoint, you can also select *File > Share* and choose from the following options:

➤ **Share with People.** If you haven't saved your presentation to One-Drive, PowerPoint will prompt you to do so before opening the Share pane, where you can enter email addresses to *Invite people* to access the file, *Send as an attachment*, or *Get a sharing link*.

> ➤ **Email.** If you don't want to save your presentation to OneDrive, you can still share it with others by email. Options include *Send as Attachment*, *Send as PDF*, and *Send as Internet Fax*. You can also *Send a Link* but must save your file in a shared location first.

If you upload the document to a cloud storage service such as OneDrive, PowerPoint will prompt you to enter the email addresses of the people you would like to share the file with. For each address, you can designate *Can Edit* (if you would like them to be able to make changes to the presentation) or *Can View* (a read-only copy). You can also enter a message to your collaborator(s) that PowerPoint will send along with a link to the shared file.

An Internet connection is required to access the shared presentation, but collaborators do not need to have a Microsoft account. Once a collaborator clicks on the link and starts editing, you can work on the document at the same time or separately. If your collaborators don't have the desktop version of PowerPoint, they can use PowerPoint Online for free. Collaboration features may not work correctly for people who are using older versions of the software.

Present Online and *Publish Slides* are options better suited for intermediate users. If you want additional information on these features, use PowerPoint's *Tell Me* tool.

Note that even if you don't use PowerPoint's collaboration features, it's still possible to email presentations back and forth and use comments. It may be old-fashioned, but it gets the job done.

Basic sharing features are also enabled from the iOS and Android versions of the PowerPoint app.

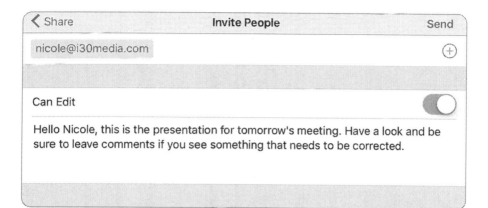

Protip: Before sharing a PowerPoint file with lots of images, audio, or video, you may want to compress the additional files it contains. This will decrease the presentation's size and improve the playback performance of any video and audio you've embedded in your slides. To do so, you'll go to *File > Info > Media Size and Performance*. Select *Compress Media* and choose the appropriate compression option. To compress static images, you will need to use the *Compress Pictures* tool on the Picture Tool Format tab as mentioned in Chapter 2.

How to add a comment

To add a comment to a PowerPoint slide in the desktop or online versions of PowerPoint, simply display the appropriate slide in the Slide Area and select the *New Comment* tool on the Insert tab. A *Comment* icon will appear on the slide. Click the Comment icon to open the Comments pane, which will be situated on the right side of your screen. From here, type your comment into the text box on the Comments pane. Press the *Enter* key on your keyboard when you are done.

You can also attach comments to specific elements within a slide. To do so, select the element before clicking the *New Comment* tool. When you're done commenting on the presentation, you can close the Comments pane by clicking *X* in the upper right corner.

If you are using the mobile PowerPoint app, the Comment icon should be visible below the slide being edited. Tap it to add your comment.

How to reply to a comment

To review and reply to a comment on a slide, click the Comment icon on it. This will open the Comments pane, where you can read the comment and, if necessary, enter a reply. Simply type your reply in the *Reply* text box and press the *Enter* key on your keyboard when done.

How to edit or delete a comment

You can edit your own comment at any time. Select the comment you want to edit within the Comments pane, make your changes, and press *Enter*. If you want to delete a comment entirely (yours or anyone else's), just select the comment on the Comments pane and click *Delete* or the "X" symbol. On the mobile app, tap the icon that looks like a speech bubble with a tiny "X" located next to the comment.

When you are ready to save a final draft of your presentation, you may want to delete all the attached comments. Doing so is easier than it sounds. Just click on the drop-down arrow below the Delete tool on the Review tab and then select *Delete All Comments and Ink in This Presentation.*

Ink refers to the results of the *Ink Annotations* tool, also found on the Review tab. It's better suited to the needs of intermediate users. However, if you want to learn more, type *ink annotations* into the Tell Me field and choose *Get help with ink annotations* for a list of helpful articles and tutorials.

Protecting a presentation

PowerPoint 2016 includes several features to protect your presentations. In Windows, they are accessed via the Info tab in the Backstage View menu. Mac users can use the Protect Presentation button on the Review Tab. Selecting *Protect Presentation* will let you:

➤ **Mark as Final** (Windows) or **Read Only** (macOS). Selecting this option will convert your presentation to read-only and prevent anyone else from making changes without creating a new copy first.

➤ **Encrypt with Password** (Windows) or **Password** (macOS). This will set a password that all users must enter to open the presentation. (Don't forget the password, or you may not be able to access your own slide deck!)

➤ **Add a Digital Signature.** If you have a digital ID, you can use this tool to add it to your presentation. Digital IDs are used to validate your identity, proving that you are the author of the presentation in question. You can purchase a digital ID from several Microsoft partners including DocuSign and GlobalSign.

➤ **Inspect Presentation.** If you want to make sure that comments and ink you may have forgotten to delete are not included before you share a presentation with others, you can use *Inspect Presentation* to check your file for hidden properties as well as personal information.

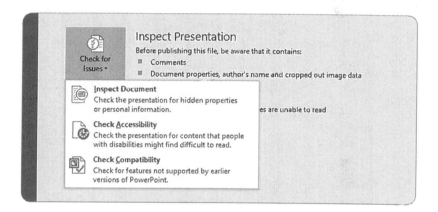

Printing, sharing, and exporting slide decks

A PowerPoint presentation never reaches its full potential until it has been shared with the world. PowerPoint 2016 gives you many options for getting your slide deck to its intended audience, from exporting it as a PDF or video, to sharing it with collaborators and printing hard copies. Let's explore the methods beginners are most likely to use.

How to print your PowerPoint

Though PowerPoint presentations are ultimately intended for viewing on a computer monitor or projection on a screen, you may occasionally want to print hard copies to distribute to your audiences or reviewers. Select *File > Print* to access your options and a preview of your presentation in Backstage View. In addition to choosing your printer and adjusting the number of copies, options include:

➤ **Print All Slides.** Prints every slide in your presentation.

➤ **Print Current Slide.** Only prints the slide you are currently previewing.

➤ **Custom Range.** Enter specific slides or ranges of slides to print.

While the default setting is to print full-page slides, you can choose to print *Notes Page*, *Outline,* or *Handouts* instead. Handouts are particularly useful if you want to give your audience members a physical copy of your presentation to refer to later. PowerPoint gives you the option to print handout pages with one to nine slides per page.

You can also print a presentation when working in PowerPoint Online. However, you'll find fewer print options. The same goes for the PowerPoint mobile apps, which may require additional steps to activate wireless printing from your device.

How to export a PowerPoint

If you want to share your PowerPoint as a PDF or video, package it for CD or flash drive, or create custom handouts, select *File > Export* for options. For hosting PowerPoint presentations online, most users export the presentation to video and then upload it to YouTube or a social media service. We'll focus on exporting to PDF and other packaging options below.

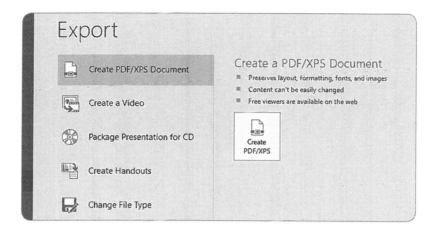

Exporting as a PDF

Whether you choose to save a copy of your presentation as a PDF using the *Save As* function or the *Create PDF Document* function at *File > Export*, the result is the same: a document in PDF format with the layout, formatting, and fonts used in your presentation preserved. Anyone with the PDF will be able to open and view the file using software that comes installed on desktop computers and mobile devices.

Whether saving or exporting as a PDF, you will need to choose a few settings in the *Publish as PDF or XPS* pop-up window, as well as choose a location to which the system will save the PDF file. If you only want a PDF of an individual slide or range of slides, you can make those changes by clicking *Options . . .* on the pop-up. Click *Publish* when you're done.

Packaging presentations for others to use

Perhaps you've created a PowerPoint slide deck for someone else. In order to present it to an audience, they will need the file as well as the linked and embedded items it contains, such as video, audio, and fonts. You can manually collect all of these items in one place, but that may be time-consuming. Instead, use *File > Export > Package Presentation for CD*.

When the *Package for CD* pop-up window opens, choose *Copy to Folder* (if you intend to save on a network drive or USB flash drive) or *Copy to CD* (if you are burning it to a CD).

Conclusion

In the past 30 minutes, you have learned how to navigate the PowerPoint user interface, create new presentations from scratch (or by using templates and themes), how to work with basic slide elements like text and pictures, and add shapes and SmartArt Graphics, charts, animations, transitions, and even cat videos (when prudent to do so). You also now know how to print, protect, share, and present your PowerPoint deck once it is complete.

Now it is time to put this knowledge to work, whether your ultimate goal is to impress potential investors with an eye-catching presentation, win an expanded department budget at the office, convince your parents of the merits of a new dog, persuade your local housing association to join your efforts to humanely care for the community's strays, or woo your dream date. Whenever you need to enhance your message with visuals, Power-Point—and *PowerPoint Basics In 30 Minutes*—will be there for you.

As always, I have enjoyed sharing my experience with you, and I hope you have found it as pleasant to read this guide as I did to write it. You can learn more about me at my website, www.thequirkycreative.com, or by looking me up on LinkedIn (www.linkedin.com/in/thequirkycreative). I would love to hear how you are doing with PowerPoint or see pictures of your cats, so please don't hesitate to drop me a line.

Thanks for reading!

P.S. If you are happy with the knowledge you have gained from *PowerPoint Basics In 30 Minutes*, please let other people know about it, either by leaving an honest review online or recommending this guide to your personal and professional networks.

Keyboard Shortcuts

Windows Shortcuts
Playback and navigation

F5 — View slide show from first slide

Shift + F5 — View slide show from current slide

Control + N — Opens new presentation file

Control + O — Open file

Control + S — Save

Control + W — Close presentation

Control + M — Insert new slide

Page Up — Move to previous slide

Page Down — Move to next slide

Control + P — Print

Control + F1 — Show/hide the Ribbon

Control + Q — Quit PowerPoint

Alt + F — Backstage View

Alt + H — Home tab

Alt + N — Insert tab

Alt + G — Design tab

Alt + P — Toggle between Play and Pause in Normal and Slide Show views

Alt + S — Slide Show tab

Alt + M — Slide Master tab

Alt + R — Review tab

Alt + W — View tab

Alt + A — Animations tab

Alt + K — Transitions tab

Alt + Q — Stop media playback in Normal and Slide Show views

Formatting and editing

Control + B — Bold text

Control + I — Italicize text

Control + U — Underline text

Control + A — Select all

Control + F — Find text

Control + H — Find and replace text, also hide pointer and navigation buttons (in Slide Show view)

Control + Shift + H — Show/hide Notes pane

Control + Z — Undo

Control + Y — Repeat or redo

Control + X — Cut selected text, formatting, or objects

Control + C — Cut selected text, formatting, or objects

Control + V — Paste copied text, formatting, or objects

Control + Shift + D — Duplicate active slide

Control + G — Group selected slide objects

Control + Shift + G — Ungroup selected slide objects

Tab — Indent text

Esc — Return to Normal view from Reading or Slide Show view

Control + E — Center-align text

Control + L — Left-align text

Control + R — Right-align text

Control + K — Insert hyperlink

Control + Left Arrow — Move cursor one word to the left, nudge selected object leftwards

Control + Right Arrow — Move cursor one word to the right, nudge selected object rightwards

Control + Up Arrow — Move cursor to the start of the previous paragraph, nudge selected object upwards

Control + Down Arrow — Move cursor to the start of the next paragraph, nudge selected object down

Control + Home — Move cursor to first word in a text box, go to the first slide in the presentation

Control + End — Move cursor to the last word in a text box, go to the last slide in the presentation

Control + Backspace — Delete one word to the left

Control + Delete — Delete one word to the right

Control + Enter — Move to next text placeholder, add new slide if no text placeholders exist

Shift + F3 — Toggle case of selected text

Control + Shift + > — Increase font size

Control + Shift + < — Decrease font size

F7 — Run spellcheck

macOS Shortcuts
Playback and navigation

Command + Shift + Return — Play slide show from first slide

Command + Return — Play slide show from the current slide

Command + N — New document

Command + O — Open file

Command + S — Save file

Command + W — Close document

Command + P — Print presentation

Command + Q — Quit

Command + Shift + N or Control + M — Insert new slide

Command + Shift + D — Make copy of the selected slide

Command + Minus Sign — Zoom out

Command + Plus Sign — Zoom in

Command + 1 — Switch to Normal view

Command + 2 — Switch to Slide Sorter view

Command + 3 — Switch to Notes Page view

Command + 4 — Switch to Outline view

Command + Shift + Return — Switch to slide show

Command + Control + F — Switch to full screen (hide menus)

Option + Return — Switch to Presenter view

Command + Option + Control + G — Show or hide guides

N, Page Down, Right Arrow, Down Arrow, or the Spacebar (or click the mouse button) — Perform the next animation or advance to the next slide

P, Page Up, Left Arrow, Up Arrow, or Delete — Return to the previous animation or Return to the previous slide

Command + Home or Command + Fn + Left Arrow — Beginning of document

Command + End or Command + Fn + Right Arrow — End of document

Esc, Command + Period, or Hyphen — End a slide show

Formatting and editing

Command + B — Bold text

Command + I — Italicize text

Command + U — Underline text

Command + A — Select all

Command + F — Find text

Command + E — Center text

Command + L — Left-align text

Command + R — Right-align text

Command + K — Insert link

Command + D — Duplicate selected objects

Command + F — Find text and formatting

Option + Left Arrow — Move cursor one word to the left

Option + Right Arrow — Move cursor one word to the right

Option + Up Arrow — Move cursor to the start of the previous paragraph

Option + Down Arrow — Move cursor to the start of the next paragraph

Command + Delete — Delete one word to the left

Command + Fn + Delete — Delete one word to the right

Command + Option + G — Group the selected objects

Command + Option + Shift + G — Ungroup the selected objects

Page Up — Up one screen

Page Down — Down one screen

Shift + F3 or Fn + Shift + F3 — Toggle case of selected text

F7 or Fn + F7 — Check Spelling

Tab — Select the next object

Shift + Tab — Select the previous object

About the author

Angela penned her first novel at the age of 11—an epic 10-page adventure involving several princesses, Yoda, and He-Man's arch nemesis, Skeletor. All six copies—meticulously inked on wide-ruled notebook paper—received critical acclaim, though to be fair, her grandmother thought it could use more character development.

After a high school literary career crafting emotionally overwrought poetry, Angela stepped away from fiction to study Journalism and Mass Communication at the University of Colorado. This was followed by more than a decade working in real estate marketing, until she founded The Quirky Creative. She now writes about careers, healthcare, business, craft beer, biotechnology, food, and a plethora of additional topics for print and digital publications, small businesses, and other clients around the world.

When she's not removing cats from her keyboard, you can find Angela searching for the perfect taco, running 5Ks, whipping up original pastry recipes, and hiking the Colorado Mountains with her photographer husband.

Angela is the author of *Microsoft Word In 30 Minutes*, *PowerPoint Basics In 30 Minutes*, and the award-winning *LinkedIn In 30 Minutes (2nd Edition)*.

Index

Introduction to Microsoft Word In 30 Minutes

The following bonus chapter is the introduction to Microsoft Word In 30 Minutes, by author Angela Rose. To download the ebook or purchase the paperback, visit the book's official website, word.in30minutes.com.

In 1985 I experienced my first broken bone.

I didn't shatter a femur skydiving, or have my rib cracked by an anaconda. Nor did the accident involve any other brave undertaking, natural disaster, or wild animal. Instead, my proximal phalanx (otherwise known as my big toe) was broken by a humble typewriter. An off-white, manual, portable typewriter from Sears, to be precise.

I had received the typewriter as a 12th birthday gift the year before, fancying myself the next great American novelist. I had a lot of fun with that typewriter, composing tales of adolescent highs and lows and attempting to emulate the storytelling styles of Erma Bombeck and Judy Bloom—my favorite authors at the time. Then I dropped the typewriter. On my foot. And it broke my big toe.

I never felt the same about typewriters after that. In fact, since adopting a personal computer complete with word processing software as my writing tool of choice more than two decades ago, I had forgotten about the typewriter. Now the most distressing inconvenience I encounter while plying my trade is my feline assistants jumping on the keyboard. But thanks to Microsoft Word, I can erase the random gibberish they insert into my documents with a quick tap of the backspace key rather than using up hours with painstaking, manual corrections.

Word also allows me to add photos, make tables and charts, and change font styles, sizes and colors with a few clicks. Checking spelling and grammar is instantaneous, and finding alternate words using the built-in thesaurus is a breeze. I can even save my documents to the cloud so others can share their comments.

Given all that, I can honestly say Microsoft Word is fahskath[b?ti[ghoiga;bsk jht[g'hhslgg'hl!

More than just a word processor

Millions of people use Microsoft Word every day. I cannot imagine working as a freelance writer without it—the program is essential to my work writing magazine articles, blog posts, website text, and even books like the one you are reading right now. But you don't have to make your living stringing words together to benefit from Microsoft Word. Almost anyone will find dozens of personal and professional uses for this versatile program.

What are people doing with Microsoft Word? Here are just a few examples:

➤ **Eve just graduated from high school and is heading off to college.** She has used Word in the past for term papers, but plans to use it a lot more this fall. From typing up lecture notes to organizing her study schedule and homework deadlines, Eve will rely on Word documents to keep her goals on track. Further, uploading files to OneDrive will allow her to access them from her PC at home, her laptop in the classroom, or even her phone when she is on the go.

➤ **Phil uses Microsoft Word every day, and has been doing so since the 1990s.** However, he's avoided upgrading until now because he doesn't want to have to relearn how to use it. He bought this book because he's worried about all the new features and wants to get up to speed on the user interface for Word 2016 as quickly as possible.

➤ **Robert has never used a word processor before.** His career as a metalworker never required it. Now he has retired and wants to record his family's history. He is slowly learning to type and plans to use Word to create documents containing his family tree, stories he heard from his grandparents, and photos of various ancestors that he has collected over the years. Once he has created a document that contains all of the text and images, Word will make it easy for him to format, print, and distribute it to relatives all over the country.

➤ **Shahida is preparing to search for a new job.** She has used Word numerous times in her current position as an office manager, but she is excited about creating an eye-catching résumé and cover letter based on the new templates in Word 2016.

➤ **Annie is writing her first book about the care and training of cats.** She is going to use Word 2016 for her Windows PC as well as Word Online to prepare her manuscript. Once she has a draft in hand, she will turn to friends and family who have offered help as proofreaders. Word's Track Changes feature will make it easy to accept or reject their suggestions.

➤ **Fernando recently subscribed to Office 365 in preparation for launching a new company.** He is currently using Word to put together a business plan complete with tables, charts and footnoted research that should impress prospective investors. Fernando will use Word's security features to ensure that only selected people will be able to review the business plan.

I have written this guide—complete with step-by-step instructions, screenshots, and plenty of cat-related anecdotes—to help all kinds of people quickly learn basic features and tools of Word 2016. It is not a comprehensive guide, and certain advanced topics are excluded. Nevertheless, *Microsoft Word In 30 Minutes* covers all of the basics as well as most intermediate-level topics, including:

➤ Navigating Word's Ribbon.

➤ How to create a new document.

➤ Formatting, styles, and themes.

➤ How to save, print, and export Word files.

➤ Easy ways to add cool elements such as images and charts.

➤ How to whip up a table of contents, indexes, and footnotes.

➤ How to make sure your copy is perfect.

➤ Collaboration and other ways to share documents.

Even better, you will learn all of this in about 30 short minutes. That is less time than most of us spend watching funny cat videos (or dog videos, if you're not into cats) on YouTube every day! We don't have any time to lose, so let's get started.

If you're interested in learning more about this title, or buying the ebook or paperback, visit the official website located at word.in30minutes.com.

Introduction to
Excel Basics
In 30 Minutes

The following bonus chapter is the introduction to Excel Basics In 30 Minutes (2nd Edition). To download the ebook or purchase the paperback, visit the book's official website, excel.in30minutes.com.

Excel:
Not Just For Nerds!

Some years ago, a colleague stopped by my cubicle and asked for help with a project he was working on. John wanted to create a long list of names, categorize them, and assign a score on a scale of one to 10 for each one. He also needed to identify the top scores and create category averages.

John knew I was familiar with all kinds of desktop and online software. He asked, "Which one would you recommend for these types of tasks?"

"That's easy," I answered. "Enter the data into Microsoft Excel or Google Sheets. You can then alphabetize the list, sort by the highest and lowest scores, and draw out category averages. You can even create neat-looking charts based on the results." I used Excel to whip up a basic list, and emailed him the file.

John thanked me profusely, but admitted, "I have only the vaguest idea about Excel and almost no experience with spreadsheets."

John's situation is not unusual. Millions of people know that Excel can be used for financial tracking and number crunching. They may have even opened Excel and entered some numbers into a corporate expense worksheet.

Nevertheless, Excel suffers from an *image problem.* Most people assume that spreadsheet programs such as Excel are intended for accountants, analysts, financiers, scientists, mathematicians, and other geeky types. Creating a spreadsheet, sorting data, using functions, and making charts seems daunting. Many think that these are tasks best left to the nerds.

I'm here to tell you that spreadsheets are not just for nerds. Almost anyone can use Excel for work, school, personal projects and other uses. I've written this guide to help you quickly get up to speed on basic concepts, using plain English, step-by-step instructions, and lots of screenshots. Thirty minutes from now, you'll know how to:

➤ Create a spreadsheet and enter numbers and text into cells.

➤ Perform addition, multiplication, and other simple mathematical functions.

➤ Derive values based on percentages.

➤ Perform timesaving tasks, such as sorting large lists and automatically applying the same formula across a range of values.

➤ Make great-looking charts.

You can imagine how these techniques can help in real-world situations, from tracking household expenses to making sales projections. You can even use them to organize events, and track the office football pool.

We only have 30 minutes, so let's get started!

If you're interested in learning more about this title, or buying the ebook or paperback, visit the official website located at excel.in30minutes.com.

Introduction to Google Drive & Docs In 30 Minutes

The following bonus chapter is the introduction to Google Drive & Docs In 30 Minutes (2nd Edition). To download the ebook or purchase the paperback, visit the book's official website, googledrive.in30minutes.com.

Why you need to use Google's free office suite

Thanks for picking up a copy of *Google Drive & Docs In 30 Minutes,* 2nd Edition. I wrote this unofficial user guide to help people get up to speed with Google's remarkable (and free) online office suite that includes file storage (Google Drive), a word processor (Google Docs), a spreadsheet program (Google Sheets), and a presentation tool (Google Slides).

How do people use these applications? There are many possible uses. Consider these examples:

> ➤ **A harried product manager needs to work on an important proposal over the weekend.** In the past, she would have dug around in her purse to look for an old USB drive she uses for transferring files. Or, she might have emailed herself an attachment to open at home. Not anymore. Now she saves the Word document and an Excel spreadsheet to Google Drive at the office. Later that evening, on her home PC, she opens her Google Drive folder to access and edit the files. All of her saves are updated to Google Drive. When she returns to work the following Monday, the updated data can be viewed at her workstation.

> ➤ **The organizer of a family reunion wants to survey 34 cousins** about attendance, lodging preferences, and potluck dinner preparation (always a challenge—the Nebraska branch of the family won't eat corn or Garbanzo beans). He emails everyone a link to an online form he created using Google Forms. Relatives open the form on their browsers, and submit their answers. The answers are automatically transferred to Sheets, where the organizer can see the responses and tally the results.

> ➤ A small business consultant is helping the owner of Slappy's Canadian Diner ("*We Put The Canadian Back In Bacon*") **prepare a slideshow for potential franchisees in Ohio**. The consultant and Slappy collaborate using Google Slides, which lets them remotely access the deck and add text, images, and other elements. The consultant shares a link to the slideshow with her consulting partner, so he can periodically review it on the Google Slides app on his phone and check for problems. Later,

Slappy meets his potential franchise operators at a hotel in Cleveland, and uses Google Slides on his iPad to pitch his business.

➤ **An elementary school faculty uses Docs to collaborate on lesson plans.** Each teacher accesses the same document from home or the classroom. Updates are instantly reflected, even when two teachers are simultaneously accessing the same document. Their principal (known as "Skinner" behind his back) is impressed by how quickly the faculty completes the plans, and how well the curriculums are integrated.

➤ At the same school, the 5th-grade teachers **ask their students to submit homework using Docs**. The teachers add corrections and notes, which the students can access at home using a Web browser. It's much more efficient than emailing attachments, and the students don't need to bug their parents to purchase Microsoft Office.

Many people are introduced to Google's online office suite through Docs, the incredibly popular online word processor. Others are attracted by the free storage and syncing features of Google Drive. Microsoft Office, which includes Word, Excel, PowerPoint, and OneDrive, can cost hundreds of dollars. While Drive is not as sophisticated as Microsoft Office, it handles basic documents and spreadsheets very well. Google Drive also offers a slew of powerful online features, including:

➤ The ability to review the history of a specific document, and revert to an earlier version.

➤ Simple Web forms and online surveys which can be produced without programming skills or website hosting arrangements.

➤ Collaboration features that let users work on the same document in real time.

➤ Offline file storage that can be synced to multiple computers.

➤ Automatic notification of the release date of Brad Pitt's next movie.

I'm just kidding about the last item. But Google Drive, Docs, Sheets, Forms, and Slides really can do those other things, and without the help of your company's IT department or the pimply teenager from down the street.

These features are built right into the software, and are ready to use as soon as you've signed up.

Even though the myriad features of Google's office suite may seem overwhelming, this guide makes it easy to get started. *Google Drive & Docs In 30 Minutes* is written in plain English, with lots of step-by-step instructions, screenshots and tips. More resources are available on the companion website to this book, *googledrive.in30minutes.com*. You'll get up to speed in no time.

The second edition of *Google Drive & Docs In 30 Minutes* covers recent interface improvements, as well as the expanded capabilities of the Google Drive, Docs, Sheets, and Slides apps for iOS and Android.

We've only got half an hour, so let's get started. If you are using a PC or laptop, please download the Google Chrome browser, which works best with Google Drive, Docs, Slides, and Sheets. Instructions for the Chromebook and the mobile apps are referenced throughout the guide.

> *If you're interested in learning more about this title, or buying the ebook or paperback, visit the official website located at googledrive.in30minutes.com.*